BUDDHISM

QUEST BOOKS
are published by
The Theosophical Society in America,
Wheaton, Illinois 60189-0270,
a branch of a world organization
dedicated to the promotion of brotherhood and
the encouragement of the study of religion,
philosophy, and science, to the end that man may
better understand himself and his place in
the universe. The Society stands for complete
freedom of individual search and belief.
In the Classics Series well-known
theosophical works are made
available in popular editions.

Cover art by Jane A. Evans

Depicting a Gupta period Buddha (Indian 4th Century A.D.)

BUDDHISM

An Outline of its Teachings and Schools

H. WOLFGANG SCHUMANN

Translated by Georg Feuerstein

This publication made possible with the assistance of the Kern Foundation

QUEST BOOKS
The Theosophical Publishing House

Wheaton, Ill. U.S.A.
Madras, India / London, England

First Quest edition 1974. Fourth Quest Printing 1993

For additional information write to: The Theosophical Publishing House, 306 West Geneva Road, Wheaton, IL 60187. Published by the Theosophical Publishing House, a department of the Theosophical Society in America.

Library of Congress Cataloging in Publication Data

Schumann, Hans Wolfgang
Buddhism; an outline of its teachings and schools

(A Quest book)
"Published under a grant from the Kern Foundation."
Bibliography: p.
1. Buddhist doctrines—Introductions. 1. Title.
BQ4132.S38 1974 294.3'4'2 74-6302
ISBN 0-8356-0452-7

Printed in the United States of America

Contents

List of Drawings and Plates

Preface

The wheel symbol of the righteous ruler (*cakkavattin*). The twenty-four-spoked wheel belongs to the lion-capital of the pillar erected in Sārnāth by Emperor Asoka in the 3rd century B.C. The edict carved in the pillar warns against schism of the monastic order. The lion-capital is today India's national coat of arms; the wheel was incorporated in the Indian national flag. As a Buddhist symbol the 'wheel of the teaching' may have eight to thirty-six spokes.

Five hundred years before the rise of Christianity there originated in India a religious doctrine which does not make a god or the gods the subject of its thinking, but concentrates on man himself as interwoven with the cosmic cycle. As its author, Siddhattha Gotama, the 'Buddha', was convinced of having revealed in this teaching a natural law, he calls it 'the law' (P: *dhamma*, Skt: *dharma*), thereby simultaneously characterising it as a rule for human behaviour. Aptly his followers chose the wheel (P: *cakka*, Skt: *cakra*) as symbol of the *dhamma*: symbol of functional unity, of pivotal standstill in movement and, in ancient India, of righteous royal rulership.

From his followers the Buddha demands self-discipline and kindness, deriving these ideals from philosophical deliberations which we are able to reconstruct from his sermons handed down in the Pāli language. To present the system of these thoughts is the task of the present book.

Soon after the Buddha's death, monastic philosophers elaborated his ideas and created systems which to this day compete with the older Buddhism for adherents. Insofar as their sources are available in Sanskrit, these systems are also described in the following pages. In other words: This book is a compendium of those teachings of Hīnayāna[1] and Mahāyāna Buddhism which originated in India; the Tantrayāna is dealt with on the basis of secondary sources. It does not take into account the history of the spread of Buddhism, its locally varying popular forms, nor its influence on the social behaviour of its followers. The theme is the doctrinal edifice and I believe that all important Buddhist ideas are touched on. On the other hand I have refrained from discussing Buddhist scholasticism. Philosophy is valuable only insofar as it provides a prop and is of consequence for the conduct of life.

The working principles were: brevity, matter-of-factness, as well as abstinence from value-judgements and comparisons with Western systems of thought. The separate treatment of the Hīna- and the Mahāyāna will show that many technical terms common to both branches differ in their meaning.

With the exception of the chapter on Tantrism, this study is based on original Indian texts, in Pāli for the Hīnayāna and

[1] The term 'Hīnayāna', 'Small Vehicle' (for crossing the stream of suffering), which was introduced by the Mahāyānins, is used throughout in a non-derogatory sense as a collective name for all pre-mahāyānic schools of Buddhism of which the Theravāda is only one. The wish of the Theravādins to stop the use of this expression which they feel to be defamatory is not realisable for want of an alternative term.

in Sanskrit for the Mahāyāna parts of the book. Indian names and terms are accordingly given partly in Pāli and partly in Sanskrit. The sources of quotations are marked by the Indian chapter and paragraph numbers as well as the volume number (in Roman numeral) and page of the printed edition.

It is a pleasant obligation to acknowledge the help I received from the Archaeological Department of the Union of Burma in producing the line drawings illustrating the text. I would also like to express my gratitude to Bhikkhu U Kassapa (Rangoon) for many talks on the *dhamma* from which I derived much valuable information and stimulation. Bhikkhu Pāsādika, M.A. (Nālandā), Bhikkhu Vimalo (Chaiya) and Lama Anagārika Govinda (Almora), were so kind as to read the typescript and to offer valuable advice. Through extensive comments, Lama Govinda has considerably enriched my vision of the Mahāyāna and Tantrayāna. That I cannot in all details subscribe to the doctrinary viewpoints of these venerable monks has its reason in the rationalistic attitude and the analytical-descriptive method of the present work, which is concerned with comprehending and systematising the Buddha's teaching and not with apologetics and missionising. Cordial thanks to all those who assisted in the making of this book, last, but not least, to Mr. Gerald Yorke, for his help in preparing the English edition.

H.W.S.

Introduction

In the West a study of Buddhism is the assignment of two disciplines: Indology and Comparative Religion. Indology has been domiciled in Germany since 1818 when the first professor's chair for Sanskrit and Indian Studies was instituted at the University of Bonn. Comparative Religion was introduced into the University curriculum by the Oxford-based German Indologist Friedrich Max Müller (1823–1900). Neither of these branches of research can make any scientifically based value-judgements about the religions under their examination. Both serve for unbiased understanding and the promotion of spiritual contacts between the cultures.

Research into Buddhism became a scientific pursuit in Europe around the middle of the nineteenth century. It is a happy illustration of international co-operation in which now one, then another country took the lead and in which around 1900 scholars from Asia and America also joined with valuable contributions. Meanwhile the secondary literature has become so voluminous and ramified that no one can undertake to read it all. The *Bibliography of Buddhism* by Shinsho Hanayama, published in 1961 in Tokyo, lists 15,073 papers and books.

In his *Bibliographie der buddhistischen Philosophie* (1950), the Swiss Indologist C. Regamey distinguishes between three schools of Buddhist research: the Anglo-German, the Leningrad and the Modern Schools.

The *Anglo-German School* confines itself to the study of Theravāda Buddhism and the Pāli sources whereby it ordinarily attributes little significance to the third and younger *piṭaka*, that of scholasticism (*Abhidhamma*). Its great merits lie in that it made the Pāli texts accessible in printed editions and produced easy-to-read presentations of the Dhamma; it is, therefore, the best-known school of interpretation whose works are still playing a leading role in Western Buddhism. It owes its name to the fact that British and German scholars did the main work in it: T. W. Rhys Davids (who founded the Pāli Text Society in London, in 1881), H. Oldenberg, E. Windisch, R. Pischel, H. Beckh, Nyānatiloka Mahāthera, K. Seidenstuecker and, in recent times, K. Schmidt. In the field of Pāli philology the German scholars Wilhelm Stede (anglicised to William Stede), W. Geiger and H. Lueders also deserve mention. A substantial contribution to Pāli research was also made by Danish scholars.

The *Leningrad School* flourished between 1920 and 1935 and is connected with the names of O. Rosenberg, Th. Stcherbatsky, and E. Obermiller. In contrast to the Anglo-German School it directed its attention particularly to the scholastic texts in both Pāli and Sanskrit. Moreover, it utilised the oral tradition in Buddhist countries—a procedure which would have appeared unscientific to the older Buddhist scholars. This method has yielded valuable results and has considerably enlarged our knowledge of Buddhist terminology. However, the extensive treatment of questions in detail makes the works of the Leningrad School difficult to read by the non-specialist.

The *Modern School* is a synthesis of the two aforementioned Schools. To clarify the Buddhist system it draws on all available sources, not only in Pāli and Sanskrit, but also in Tibetan, Chinese and Japanese, and furthermore includes archaeological evidence. Since it is concerned with gaining knowledge on, and insight into, the whole of Buddhism, it devotes equal attention to the Hīnayāna and the Mahāyāna.

The most important of the older works of the Modern School were written by French and Belgian scholars, which is why it is often referred to as the Franco-Belgian School, L. de la Vallée Poussin should be regarded as its past master. Other great French and Belgian names are: S. Lévi, A. Foucher, A. Bareau and—last but not least—É. Lamotte, to whom we owe the most comprehensive standard work of this School (*Histoire du Bouddhisme Indien*, Louvain 1958).

One must, however, not be misled by the designation Franco-Belgian School. Indian and Japanese scholars have as much a part in it as England's E. Conze, Italy's G. Tucci, Austria's E. Frauwallner, and the German Indologists M. Walleser, H. Waldschmidt, H. von Glasenapp and H. Bechert. The present compendium of the Buddhadhamma as well has to be counted in the Modern School as it portrays the Hīnayāna, of which the Theravāda is the most important offspring, and the Mahāyāna with equal benevolence.

No representative of the Modern School would deny the factual differences—comparable to those between Protestantism and Catholicism in the West—which exist between Theravāda, Mahāyāna and Tantrayāna. However, by its works the School reveals the unbroken line of two and a half thousand years' development: it shows the close logical relationship between the earlier and the later branches of Buddhism. Towards the end of the last century, Western Buddhist scholars occasioned through their works a revival of Buddhism in Asia. Perhaps the Modern School could today contribute to bringing the Theravāda and the Mahāyāna closer together.

What effect scientifically based publications on Buddhism can have is borne out by the fact that of the 2000–3000 Buddhist followers in West Germany the greater number discovered the Buddha's doctrine through the objective representations of Indologists and scholars of comparative religion. Apparently there is more persuasive power in critical studies than in books with missionary intent.

I

THE BUDDHA'S LIFE

In 1882 a French scholar published a book in which he tried to prove that the man bearing the honorary title of '*Buddha*' has never lived. The accounts linked with the 'Enlightened' or 'Awakened One' in his opinion are unhistorical and nothing but a new infusion of the old nature myth of the solar hero.

This theory is all the more surprising since in the previous year, 1881, a book had been published which put the historicity of the Buddha beyond all doubt: the work *Buddha—sein Leben, seine Lehre, seine Gemeinde* by the Goettingen Professor Hermann Oldenberg (1854–1920). Textual and archaeological evidence which has come to light since then has fully confirmed and completed the picture sketched by Oldenberg of the life of the great Indian.

Ṣiddhattha Gotama, the 'Buddha', was born a contemporary of Thales, Anaximander, Pythagoras and Laotse, probably in the year 563 B.C. This date has been arrived at by calculating back from the fairly well-secured life-data of the Indian emperor Asoka (sole ruler 269 B.C., coronation 265, death 232), who, as a Ceylonese chronicle states, was crowned 218 years after the death of the octogenarian Buddha; a possible error of ± 10 years has, however, to be admitted. All European researchers reject the tradition current in Theravādic countries according to which Gotama was born in 624 B.C. and died in 544 B.C.

The canonical Pāli scriptures supply reliable information about the later years of Gotama's life. However, what we know of his youth stems from later texts and commentaries, from whose tangled mass of legends the historical kernel must be separated.

According to this later tradition, Māyā, Siddhattha's mother is said to have set out from the home of her husband in Kapilavatthu in order to give birth to her baby in the house of her parents in Devadaha. But on the way, in a grove of Sāla trees near the village of Lumbinī (230 km North of Benares in modern Nepāl), the boy was born, some Easterners assume by Caesarean section.[2]

Mother and child were taken back to Kapilavatthu where the mother died one week later. Suddhodana, the father, then entrusted his son to the sister of the deceased woman, his second wife, Mahāpajāpatī, who reared him affectionately.

The family of the coming Buddha bore the name of Gotama and belonged to the tribe of the *Sakiya*[3] of the warrior caste (*khattiya*). At the time of his son's birth the country squire Suddhodana was governor (rāja) of a province in the kingdom of Kosala—an office for which elections were held among the nobility at regular intervals. The title '*Rāja*' for the holder of this position has led Buddhist tradition to regard the Buddha as a prince. Text passages which refer to Suddhodana's tilling his fields were explained away by the assumption of an agricultural festival at which the king had to ceremoniously plough a furrow.

Siddhattha's youth was free from material worries. The region around Kapilavatthu is fertile, in particular for rice, and offers its inhabitants a good livelihood. The scenery is also charming. In clear weather the southern slopes of the Himālayas stand out against the skyline while scattered groups of trees throw patches of shadow on the field-covered plain.

Siddhattha's education, which apparently did not include reading and writing, was in keeping with tradition among the ancient Indian nobility. He was married at sixteen and at twenty-nine had a son whom he called Rāhula. In the same year he was overcome by a radical change which he later described to his monks as follows:

[2] This assumption finds support in Buddhist art which represents the mother giving birth to the child out of her right hip. But the fact that such an operation would have been performed in a house, speaks against it.

[3] In the Pāli texts occasionally also spelled *Sakya* and *Sakka*.

I, too, . . . have formerly . . . , myself subject to birth, searched for that which is subject to birth, subject to old age, illness, death, sorrow, defilement, looked exactly for that which is subject (to all that). Then . . . I realised: Why do I . . . who am subject (to all this), seek exactly that which is subject to (this)? Should I not, after recognising misery in birth (etc.), search for the unborn, ageless, non-ill, deathless, griefless, undefiled, unexcelled, burden-free extinction (*nibbāna*)? Soon thereafter, young (as I was), having shorn off my hair and beard (and) donned the yellow robes, against the wish of my weeping . . . parents, I went from home into homelessness. (M 26 I p. 163)

He further reports that he became a disciple of a teacher named Āḷāra Kālāma. It was not long before he had understood Āḷāra's teaching but he recognised that it did not lead to liberation. With a second teacher, Uddaka Rāmaputta, he underwent a similar experience. Therefore, he also turned away from him and set out upon his wanderings.

In the vicinity of the village Uruvelā, the modern Bodh-Gayā (210 km South-East of Benares), Siddhattha discovered a spot convenient for his religious practices. There, on the river Nerañjarā (today: Nīlājanā), a tributary of the Phalgu, he settled down to the most stringent asceticism. For six long years he exposed himself to self-mortifications, practised difficult breathing exercises and abstained from taking sufficient food. Five ascetics gathered around him in the hope that 'the truth (*dhamma*) which the ascetic Gotama might find, he will expound to us' (M 36 I p. 247). But when Siddhattha realised that self-torture is no way to deliverance, he ceased his asceticism and again took proper nourishment. The five fellow-ascetics thereupon regarded him an apostate and abandoned him.

Left again to himself, he suddenly recollected an experience of his youth:

I remember(ed) how, sitting in the shadow of a Jambu-tree

For five centuries the artists of India desisted from depicting the Buddha; his presence was only indicated by symbols. Only in the 1st century A.D.—simultaneously in Mathurā and the hellenised Gandhāra—the scruples were dropped and the master became a favourite motif of pictorial art.

In the course of time the positions of the hands and body were standardised. A famous sculpture of the Gupta period (5th century), found in Sārnāth, depicts the master in the gesture of setting the wheel of the doctrine in motion; his legs are crossed in the lotus posture. The ear-lobes are elongated from the bearing of heavy jewellery, which Gotama discarded when setting out for a homeless life. They so symbolise renunciation.

> while my father Sakka worked the furrows, I have rested free from desires, free from unwholesome emotions, after I had reached the joyful-happy first (stage of) trance connected with thinking and pondering, resulting from seclusion. (I asked myself): Should this be the path to enlightenment? (M 36 I p. 246)

Sitting under an Assattha (or: Pippala), a poplar-fig tree, he began to meditate methodically, and with his spiritual eye pierced layer after layer of the nature of existence. He remembered his previous existences, saw through the law of rebirth as a consequence of deeds (*kamma*) and realised: This is suffering, this is its origin, this is its termination and this is the way to its termination. He gained the insight:

> Unshakable is my liberation (from suffering); this is the last birth, there is (for me) no more re-existence. (M 26 I p. 167)

At that moment of the year 528 B.C.—as tradition says the first full-moon night of the month Vesākha (April–May)—Siddhattha Gotama obtained enlightenment (*bodhi*) and became a *Buddha*. He was then thirty-five years old.

Occasionally one is told that the enlightenment of the Buddha is a literary fiction, for many features of his teaching are already traceable in pre-Buddhist thought, especially in the Upaniṣads. Although this is correct, it is in fact not proof. Gotama's *bodhi* was an experience in which adopted elements of thought and convictions arrived at in contradiction to current philosophies (like the *anatta* doctrine) suddenly merged into one organic 'system'. Learned and self-found knowledge crystallised in him, revealing to him the secrets of life. In its consequences, the Buddha's enlightenment marks one of the great hours in the history of mankind.

The decision as to whether he should keep his knowledge to himself or impart it to the world seems to have cost the young Buddha considerable inner struggle. In the end his 'compassion for the unliberated, suffering beings' won, and he decided to take up teaching.

As, in the meantime, his two teachers had passed away, he wandered to the Deer Park of Isipatana (Sārnāth) near Benares in order to open the 'gate to liberation' for his former friends, the five fellow-ascetics. When they saw the alleged apostate approach, they agreed to refuse him the customary greetings. Overpowered, however, by his radiating certainty of liberation, they were unable to do so. They welcomed him, and Gotama preached to them his first sermon (= S 56, 11), called 'The Setting in Motion of the Dhamma Wheel'. For the first time he imparted to an audience his realisation of the truth of suffering and of self-discipline free from extremes as the instrument for emancipation. The 'Middle Way', which he expounded, quickly found understanding. Very soon the five ascetics accepted the teaching (*dhamma*) and became

Gotama's first monk-disciples. Before long, they became saints.

The expressions 'monk' and 'monastic order' (*saṅgha*) are not to be understood according to the Christian model. Although Buddhist monks (*bhikkhu*) differ from worldlings in their shaven heads, their yellow robes and the observation of special rules of conduct, they have not committed themselves to life-long monastic existence. There are certain formalities for ordination as well as a lengthy noviciate, but to leave the order it is sufficient to take off the robe. Ordination, incidentally, is by no means a precondition to attaining the goal; it merely facilitates the way to liberation. The Pāli canon mentions twenty lay-followers (*upāsaka*) who became saints without ever having worn the robe.

A few months after its establishment the order already had a total of sixty members. At this time the Buddha summoned his monks and exhorted them to go out to teach and encourage people to lead a pure life:

> Go ye forth, monks, for the good of the many, for the benefit of the many, out of compassion for the world, for the profit, for the good, for the benefit of gods and men. Let not two of you go together! Expound, monks, the teaching which is good in the beginning, good in the middle, good in the end, in the spirit (as also) in the letter. Show a fulfilled, pure life of virtue. There are beings who are born with little defilement; if they do not hear the teaching, they are doomed. They will understand the teaching.
>
> (Mv 11, 1 Vin I p. 21)

This is how the missionary activity of Buddhism began.

Like his monks, the Buddha, too, set out to impart the truth he had realised to a greater circle of people. He spent the next forty-five years wandering and preaching in Northern India. Only during the rainy season (June–September), which he used to pass withdrawn in a monastery, did he permit himself to rest.

The teaching alone cannot explain the extraordinary missionary success of Buddhism. Gotama himself considered it as 'profound, difficult to grasp, difficult to penetrate, factual, supreme, inaccessible to (mere) logic, subtle, intelligible only to the educated' (M 26 I p. 167). Its practical and rational approach avoiding all extremes, its cultlessness which liberated from the tyranny of the ritual which was the domain and source of income of a pretentious brahmanical priesthood; furthermore the fact that the Buddha directed his monks to teach the doctrine not in Sanskrit but in *his* language (Cv 5, 33, 1 Vin II p. 139), i.e. probably the Māgadhī dialect as the idiom of the district where he lived—all this contributed more to its diffusion than its complicated doctrinal contents. An important role was also played by the fact that his monks predominantly led a life of self-restraint. Finally it was the character of the Buddha himself that attracted followers. He was a man of harmonious, self-contained personality with great magnetism. The majesty of his appearance, his courtesy also towards people of lower status and his noble manners impressed even those who rejected his teaching.

The Pāli sources portray the character of the Buddha very clearly. His behaviour was directed by his certainty of being liberated, his contemplative temperament and kind-heartedness towards all mankind.

The self-confidence of the Buddha resulting from his liberation becomes obvious at that moment after his enlightenment when he meets the five ascetics and expounds to them his insights. Since they were unable to deny him salutation, they addressed him by name and called him 'friend'. But Gotama objected to this address:

> Monks, do not address the Thus-Come (*tathāgata*)[4] by name and by the appellation 'friend'! A saint (*arahant*), monks, is the Thus-Come, a Fully Enlightened One (*sammāsambuddha*).
>
> (M 26 I p. 171)

[4] The designation *Tathāgata*, 'He who thus Came' for the Buddha was later also used in contexts where it is meaningless. In these cases, the word will be translated 'the Perfect One'.

Enlightened and liberated, Gotama felt himself to be totally different from undelivered beings. Once (A 4, 36, 2 II p. 38) a brahmin asked him whether he was a god, a heavenly being, a spirit or a man. To all these possibilities he answered in the negative. The imperfections, which place a person into any of those categories, had been exterminated in him; he was a *Buddha.*

With this self-understanding, it is admirable that he did not handle in a doctrinary way the teaching which can transform a man to such a degree. On the contrary, he stressed that no teaching should ever be accepted on the strength of tradition, of being handed down in holy scriptures, of being in agreement with one's own views or because of trust in an authority. It should only be accepted when one has recognised it as wholesome (A 3, 65, 3 I p. 189).

Not only did Gotama abstain from pressing anyone to embrace his doctrine, he even warned against too hurried a conversion. When General Sīha, a professor of the Jain religion, after a talk with him wanted to become his follower, the master admonished him to think it over. When Sīha repeated his request for conversion, he told him to continue giving alms to the Jain monks (Mv 6, 31, 10 f. Vin I p. 236).

Gotama's ability to move people by words appears to have been extraordinary. To simple minds he spoke plainly about good deeds which would lead to rebirth in heaven. The most frequent figure of speech in such sermons is the confrontation: Of the imperfect with the Perfect One, of the evil with the virtuous, of worldly discord with the peace of liberation, etc.

That the rules of conduct, which he preached, were conclusions drawn from philosophical insights was something he only showed to those of his listeners whom he credited with openmindedness and intelligence. In this he was unconcerned about whether the listener was a lay-follower, a monk or an adherent of another religion. He did not have the closed 'fist of the teachers' who distinguish between an inner and outer, that is an esoteric and exoteric, aspect of their teaching (D 16, 2, 25 II p. 100).

The logical methods applied in the sermons of the Buddha as well as in all other early Buddhist texts are not too numerous. The sixth century B.C. did not yet know of theoretical logic. Antagonistic doctrines were mostly refuted by uncovering their absurd consequences; the basic doctrine or idea was thus proved untenable. In support of their own teachings, the Buddhist texts make use of similes, gradation, bordering-in and conditional derivation.

(1) The first-mentioned method is logically unassuming, but effective through the image-making power of the similes. These are taken from all realms of nature and Indian everyday life and prove that Gotama observed his surroundings with watchful eyes. His fame as an orator is largely the result of the vividness of his metaphors.

(2) The proof by gradation enumerates things or modes of conduct in such a way that each following thing surpasses the one preceding, and the final one, which is fulfilled in the Buddha's teaching, is recognised as outdoing them all: A is bad; B is better than A; C is better than B; . . . Z, which is held or taught by the Buddha, is best and excels all the others.

(3) The method of proof by bordering-in presupposes the dialogue as a literary form in which, of course, the second person's only role is that of a yes-and-no-man. By questions about the thinkable extremes the sphere of reasonable opinions is demarcated in both directions, and the doctrinal view of the Buddha is then characterised as lying in the middle: 'Is (the extreme) A correct, venerable So-and-so?'—'No, Sir.'—'Is (the extreme) Z correct?'—'No, Sir.'—'Hence it is correct (according to *my* teaching) to accept (the middle value) M?'—'Yes, Sir.'

(4) Conditional derivations do not occur very often in Buddhist texts; but where they appear, they bear considerable weight. It is noteworthy that each link in the chain is considered only as a partial precondition—precisely as a *conditio*—of the respective following link, not as its sole originating

factor (*causa*). The logical form of such derivations is: When A (and the other required factors) exist, then B arises; when B (and the other required factors) exist, then C arises; and so on. Sometimes the same method is used retrograde, in an analytical way: Where Z is, there must be (among others) Y as precondition; where Y is, there must be (among others) X as precondition; and so on.

Of particularly intellectual attractiveness are the conversations which the master had with brahmins and Jains. They give testimony to the intellectual flexibility of both parties and on the part of the Buddha to occasional irony. The *Majjhimanikāya* reports how he told his monks of a discussion he had with some Jains about the use of penance. Smilingly he pointed out that the Jain monks who today suffered self-inflicted tortures must have, in a previous existence, been rogues to have kammically deserved these torments. However, if one were to assume that the world was made by a creator or that it had arisen accidentally, then it would be just the Jains who must be regarded as the work of a sinister creator or the product of an adverse chance-happening (M 101 II p. 222).

As participant in a discussion, the Buddha distinguished himself through equanimity and matter-of-factness. The Jain monk Saccaka Aggivessana, who was known to be a shrewd disputant, praised him at the end of a debate because 'the colour of his face had stayed light'. Other religious teachers would have become angry during such a talk and tried to prevaricate or evade the subject (M 36 I p. 250). Gotama is thus described as a man of controlled temperament who did not get flushed.

In one matter, however, his patience was limited: When it came to the exegesis of his teaching. He accepted its rejection with composure, but severely opposed its defective understanding and misinterpretation. The monk Sāti, for example, thought he could understand it in such a way that consciousness (*viññāna*) after the death of its bearer transmigrates to the next embodiment. The master took him to task: 'From whom, you fool, have you heard that the teaching was expounded by me in this way? Have I not, you fool, in many ways declared

A legend which is probably close to the truth reports that during his daily morning alms-round the Buddha was once refused food with the argument that only he who ploughs the ground can claim food. The master thereupon touched the earth with his right hand to call upon her to testify that a spiritual teacher, too, has a right to live. He did not, however, accept the offering then made. (Tibetan wood-cut.)

that consciousness arises in dependence (and, therefore, perishes in death)?' (M 38 I p. 258). This is Gotama's most vehement behaviour reported in the Pāli sources.

All his civility with people, all his rhetorical talent, all his sincerity and education would not have sufficed to make Gotama popular to his contemporaries, had they not in his utterances felt true kindness of heart. It was not the chummy type of friendliness—it was, rather, kindness that stemmed from the distance of a superior mind and from a joyous feeling of liberation. It was kindness out of deep-felt compassion for the suffering beings of the world.

What was Gotama's daily life like?—He was one of the itinerant monks so numerous in India, with no other property than the eight permissible requisites: Three robes, alms bowl, razor, a needle, a girdle, and a waterstrainer. Walking silently from house to house in the early morning he collected the food ration for the day; then, after a brief morning meal, he and the monks accompanying him would continue their wandering. When they encountered open-minded people he would stop to answer their questions and to expound to them the teaching. Before the sun reached the zenith, they would rest at a pleasant place and eat up the remains of the alms food. Afternoon and evening would be reserved for quiet meditation and the instruction of the monks. Often he accepted the invitation of a well-wisher for a forenoon meal or for a night's lodging in his house.

A sacrifice which the Buddha made for spreading the Dhamma was to forgo the solitude which he loved. All the time he was surrounded by disciples, and his wanderings were planned in such a way that the itinerary touched well-populated places. With the help of statements in the Pāli texts the routes can be approximately reconstructed.

There are four cities in the middle of Northern India—Kosambī (50 km South-West of Allahabād), Sāvatthi (225 km North of Allahabād), Vesālī (now Basarh, 40 km North of Patna), and Rājagaha (near the modern Rājgir, 80 km South of Patna) which he visited most frequently and in which he stayed longest. Most of the smaller places where he gave sermons are either on or very near to the routes which connect these four cities. At that time the area belonged to the kingdoms of Kosala and Magadha; today it is part of the Indian states of Uttar Pradesh and Bihar.

The missionary success of the Buddha did not stop with his family. His son Rāhula, his half-brother Nanda, his nephew Ānanda, and more distant relatives like Anuruddha, Bhaddiya and Devadatta decided to become ordained as monks, while his father and his former wife became lay-followers. After long hesitation he granted his step- and fostermother Mahāpajāpatī, who had repeatedly requested it, permission to become a nun and to found an order of nuns which, however, died out in the tenth century A.D. With the exception of Devadatta, who even made attempts on the Buddha's life, only good is reported of all the Dhamma followers of the Sakiya clan.

For the reader of the Pāli canon some persons of Gotama's

entourage gain life and colour. His chief disciples were Sāriputta—a man of outstanding intellect—and Moggallāna, who is said to have possessed magical powers. Both died before the Buddha and their relics are enshrined in Sāñci. Subhūti was a master in meditation, while Mahākassapa distinguished himself in ascetic observances. It was he who convened the First Council after Gotama's death.

Among the lay-followers, too, there are some persons who stand out from the multitude. The wealthy merchant Sudatta 'Anāthapiṇḍika' (*Feeder of the Poor*) donated the Jetavana monastery in Sāvatthi, the matron Visākhā the Pubbārāma monastery in the same town. The Buddha is said to have spent altogether twenty-seven rainy seasons in these Vihāras. In Rājagaha, King Bimbisāra of Magadha ordered the Veḷuvana monastery to be built where the Buddha took residence for five or six monsoon periods. From Vesālī should be mentioned the courtesan Ambapālī, famous for her beauty, who presented a monastery to the Buddha not long before his final extinction. Scarcely less enthusiastic but less well-to-do lay-followers had to be content with occasionally feeding the master and his disciples.

An order of wandering monks which draws followers from all strata of the population is understandably regarded as a possible political factor by the ruler of the country. The rulers of Kosala and Magadha, the kings Pasenadi and Bimbisāra (who were related by marriage), had formed a favourable opinion about the Buddha, surely not least of all because they had recognised the political harmlessness of his teaching. The master was friendly with both kings and more than once they came to seek his counsel or instruction about the Dhamma. As mentioned before, the order owned monasteries in Sāvatthi, the capital of Kosala, and in Rājagaha, the capital of Magadha. That the benevolence of the two rulers promoted the spread of Buddhism is beyond all question. Also the Indian merchants who welcomed a tolerant religion which disregards caste restrictions have contributed much to the diffusion of the Dhamma. However, Buddhism became a world religion only 250 years later, when the Maurya emperor Asoka, who ruled India about the middle of the third century B.C., sent missionaries not only to all parts of his country, but also to the neighbouring states.

In the year 492 or 491 B.C. the Buddha almost fell victim to a plot for his murder. The monk Devadatta, who was his cousin as well as his brother-in-law, suggested that he entrust him, Devadatta, with the leadership of the order whereas he, the Buddha, should retire in view of his advanced age. As the master rejected this, Devadatta approached the prince Ajātasattu, son of the Magadha king Bimbisāra, to whose plans for conquests his father's friendship with the peace-loving Buddha was obstructive. Devadatta managed to persuade Ajātasattu to have the Buddha murdered. A soldier was sent to kill him, but when he came face to face with the master, he was unable to execute the order. He fell at Gotama's feet, disclosed his commission and, as the story goes, embraced the Buddha's teaching (Cv 7, 3, 6–7).

A second attempt at murder, this time through stoning, likewise failed; only Gotama's foot was wounded (Cv 7, 3, 9). In a third attempt, a mad elephant was let loose on the Buddha. Radiating loving-kindness (*mettā*) towards the animal, Gotama appeased him and escaped unhurt (Cv 7, 3, 11–12).

Since Devadatta failed to seize command of the Saṅgha, he founded his own order with stricter rules. In vain had the Buddha tried to argue him out of the idea by pointing out that ascetic practices are useless for liberation. Devadatta's order soon fell into decay.

The Buddha died at the age of eighty. While spending the monsoon season in the village of Beluva, he fell ill, but suppressed the trouble by will-power. When the monk Ānanda, who had been his personal attendant for twenty-five years, remarked that he probably did not wish to depart before he had named his successor, the aged teacher replied:

> What, Ānanda, does the order expect of me? I have, Ānanda, expounded the teaching without distinguishing an

The Buddha expounding the Dhamma. Thumb and ring-finger of his right hand form the wheel of the teaching. (After a Japanese hanging scroll of the 12th century.)

> inside and outside... Therefore, Ānanda, be islands unto yourselves, a refuge unto yourselves; take the teaching as island, the teaching as refuge, have no other refuge!
>
> (D 16, 2, 25–26 II p. 100)

The teaching (*dhamma*) and not a teacher is the supreme authority in Buddhism.

Accompanied by a group of monks, Gotama wandered to Pāvā where he took rest in the mango grove of the blacksmith Cunda. After the meal he fell ill with dysentery, but in spite of his weakened condition continued his journey to Kusināra (today: Kasia, 55 km East of Gorakhpur), where Ānanda prepared a couch for him in the shadow of some Sāla trees. When Ānanda burst into tears because of the imminent death of the master, he consoled him thus:

> Enough (of it), Ānanda, do not grieve, nor lament. Have I not always told you that all things dear and pleasant are subject to change, loss, instability? How (else) could it be here? That that which was born, has come into being, has been effected (*saṅkhata*—by the deeds of previous births as

> a new form of existence) and is subject to decay—that this should not perish is impossible. (D 16, 5, 14 II p. 144)

For the last time he admonished his monks:

> Now, monks, I exhort you: the components of the personality (*saṅkhāra*)[5] are subject to decay; exert yourselves with diligence! (D 16, 6, 7 II p. 156)

These were the Buddha's last words. Shortly afterwards he fell into a coma—described by the Sutta as a meditational state—and proceeded from this into *parinibbāna*, the state of liberation from suffering after the body is cast off.

The year of Gotama's death was 483 B.C. Greece at that time was fighting the Persian wars (which three years later were decided by Themistokles' sea victory at Salamis), while Heraclitus, Parmenides, Aeschylus, and in China Confucius, were alive.

Gotama's body was cremated one week after his passing away. The ashes were divided up and handed over to seven families of the Indian nobility, as well as to a brahmin for burial. One more noble family received ashes from the funeral pile, and the brahmin Doṇa, who had conducted the cremation ceremony, took the vessel in which the ashes of the deceased had been collected. All recipients of relics enshrined their shares in burial mounds (*thūpa*, Skt.: *stūpa*).

The *thūpa*, which was probably erected by the family of the Buddha on top of their share of the relics, was discovered and opened in 1898 in Piprāvā near Kapilavatthu, Gotama's home town. Three metres underneath its top, a small urn with oblations was found, five and a half metres deeper a stone case containing five vessels.[6] One of these, an urn made of steatite,

[5] cf. p. 80, fn. 18.

[6] All findings except the ashes are today in the *Indian National Museum*, Calcutta. Many decades ago, the ashes were handed over to the King of Thailand (Siam). Archaeologists regard the line on the urn as the oldest extant inscription of India.

Lumbinī (in Nepāl), the birth-place of the Buddha. The temple erected on older foundations in the 19th century contains in a main room in the basement a worn stone relief dating perhaps from the time of Asoka, which depicts Siddhattha being born out of the right hip of his mother who holds fast to a branch of a (Sāla-) tree. After the birth mother and child are said to have been bathed in the pool in the foreground. The pillar on the left was erected by the emperor Asoka in 245 B.C.; through it Lumbini was rediscovered in 1896. The pillar bears the inscription:

> Twenty years after his coronation king Devānapiya Piyadasi (= Asoka) came to this place and paid his respects because the Buddha, the Sage of the Sakya Clan, was born here. He ordered a stone relief and a stone pillar to be erected in order to show that the Exalted One was born here. He exempted the village Lumbinī from taxation and (reduced) the payment in kind (from the usual quarter) to one-eighth.

In spite of its tax exemption Lumbinī (now: Rummindei) could not develop

because of the swampy area to the North of the village. It consists of fifteen bamboo huts and is the terminal of a busline from Naugarh (India).

Above: The Asoka pillar of Lumbinī, over 6·50 m high. The longitudinal crack was probably caused by a lightning-stroke. The Chinese pilgrim Hsuan-tsang, who visited Lumbinī in the 7th century, found the upper part of the pillar with its capital in the form of a horse broken off and the village deserted.

The Mahābodhi temple and the Bodhi tree in Bodh-Gayā. The temple which is 48 m high, is erected above several smaller shrines. It was built in the 2nd century A.D., enlarged in the 8th century, complemented by the corner towers in the 14th and restored in the 19th century.
The Assattha tree (on the left), worshipped by pious pilgrims as the tree under which the Buddha obtained enlightenment (*bodhi*), is a grandchild of the original Bodhi tree which was destroyed in the beginning of the 7th century by the śivaitic Bengal king Śaśāṅka. The subsequent tree fell victim to a storm in 1876. The present tree is a shoot of the offspring of the original tree which the emperor Asoka in the 3rd century B.C. presented to the king of Ceylon and which still is in leaf there in the old royal city of Anurādhapura.

bears an inscription in Brāhmī script and Māgadhī language:

> This urn with relics of the exalted Buddha from the Sakiya (clan) is a donation of Sukiti and his brothers together with sisters, sons and wives.

More relics of the Buddha were found in 1958 in the area of the former city of Vesālī where in a *thūpa* a small bowl with lid, containing bone remains, ashes and gift enclosures, was discovered.[7] Presumably this is the share of relics which the noble family of the Licchavis, whose capital was Vesālī, received after Gotama's cremation.

[7] Now in the care of the *Department of Archaeology and Museums*, Government of Bihar, Patna 15.

II

HĪNAYĀNA—THE BUDDHISM OF LIBERATION THROUGH SELF-EFFORT

Councils and Sources

The canon in Pāli, on which our knowledge of early Buddhism is mainly based, was compiled and edited by three monastic councils. The First Council assembled just a few months after the Buddha's death (483 B.C.) in Rājagaha, the Second about a hundred years later (around 383 B.C.) in Vesālī, and the Third in the year 225 B.C. in Pāṭaliputta (today: Patna).

Some Western writers have questioned the historicity of the First Council, probably wrongly. For what is more natural than that the disciples of a religious pioneer meet after his death and deliberate on what ought to be done now. And since the master had appointed the teaching and not a teacher as the authority, the obvious thing was to recapitulate his sermons and to put them together to form a 'canon'. The Suttapiṭaka is said to have been recited by Ānanda, the former personal attendant of the Buddha, the Vinayapiṭaka by the monk Upāli, once the barber of the Sakiyas who had become expert in monastic procedure. We do not know exactly how the original canon was worded, as in ancient India instructions were not written down but transmitted orally.

The Second Council is responsible for the inclusion of sermons and poems by monks and nuns into the canon and for the screening of the material. Divergent utterances of Gotama from the four and a half decades of his teaching activity were harmonised, for to admit a development of his thinking and knowledge was (and still is) ruled out by the monks: According to their orthodox view, in the enlightenment experience which made him a Buddha, he had conceived the teaching complete in its final form. Also, where in the texts a key-word occurred which elsewhere was treated more elaborately, the longer section was incorporated into the shorter one—a procedure which accounts for the present length of the canon and its numerous repetitions.

The Third Council finally revised the texts anew and added to the two older Piṭakas scholastic works whose number increased during the following two centuries until the Abhidhammapiṭaka had come into existence.

Soon after the Second Council during which the Buddhist order had split into different schools, there arose several canons of texts differing from each other both in language and subject division. The canon in Pāli which belongs to the Theravāda school was for a long time handed down orally. It was only committed to writing in Ceylon towards the end of the first century B.C. The Pāli canon alone has remained preserved complete. Of all the other equally ancient collections of texts, we possess, if anything at all, mere fragments.

Although the Pāli canon as the scripture of only one Buddhist school possesses not more than partial authority, it is nevertheless a reliable source for the study of the early Buddhist system. Comparisons with extant fragments of other canons have shown that the divergencies between them do not concern the central doctrines and that the Vinaya- and the Suttapiṭaka contain chiefly old material, including, no doubt, utterances of the Buddha himself. These, of course, are in translation, as not Pāli but Māgadhī appears to have been the master's mother tongue. Some verses of the canon which are unintelligible and metrically halting in Pāli become clear and rhythmical when re-translated into Māgadhī. Both languages belong to the Middle-Indian group of dialects and are cognate to Sanskrit in a pre-classical form called Vedic.

A question frequently posed is how far the ideas contained in the two old Pāli *piṭakas* derive from the Buddha and how far from his monks. One ought by no means to conclude from the maturity of the canonical system that it already represents a development of the 'original teaching'. A man who has devoted forty-five years of his life to his teaching has had time enough to elaborate his system, to recognise contradictions and remove them, to re-examine intuitive insights soberly and to think objections over. Several corrections of thought and leaps of understanding are still demonstrable in the texts in spite of the attempts of several councils to harmonise them. Why should we doubt that the Buddha, whose moral and mental superiority was praised by his contemporaries, personally designed and erected the thought-structure which goes by his name? The monks compiled, edited and later revised and supplemented the Pāli canon. To ascribe to them central elements of the system, and accordingly to assume that pre-canonical Buddhism was essentially different from Pāli Buddhism, is sheer speculation.

The Pāli canon is divided into three collections called 'baskets' (*piṭaka*). This expression arises from the fact that the texts which were engraved or written on dried palm leaves were kept in wicker baskets, each basket comprising those books which by their topic belong together.

The first Piṭaka, the Vinayapiṭaka, contains the rules for monastic discipline (*vinaya*), the second, the Suttapitaka, the sermons (*sutta*) of the Buddha and his monks. It is subdivided into five collections (*nikāya*):

Dīghanikāya	Collection of long *suttas*;
Majjhimanikāya	Collection of medium-long *suttas*;
Saṃyuttanikāya	Collection of *suttas* grouped according to topics;
Aṅguttaranikāya	Collection of *suttas* in gradual order (according to the number of treated topics);
Khuddakanikāya	Collection of smaller texts.

The *Khuddakanikāya* consists of fifteen individual works. *Udāna* (Sayings) and *Itivuttaka* (Thus is said) contain utterances

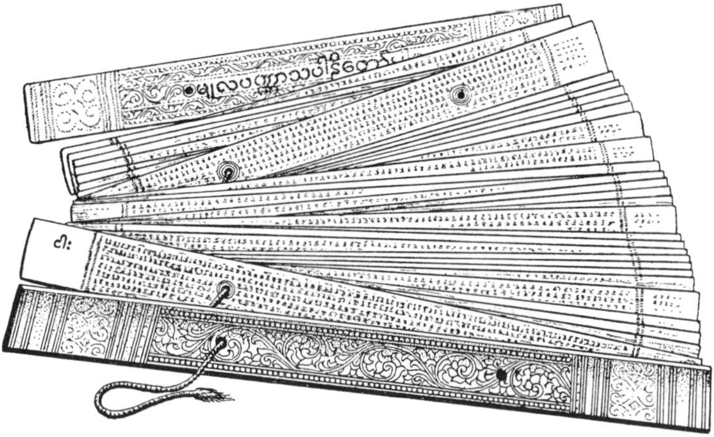

A Burmese palm-leaf manuscript of a Pāli text (Majjhimanikāya), page size 520 × 55 mm. The covers are gilded. Two cords (the right one is removed) are passed through the covers and pages and hold the book together.

of the Buddha himself, while those of his followers are in the *Dhammapada* (Path of the Doctrine), *Suttanipāta* (Sutta-fragments), *Thera- and Therīgāthā* (Stanzas by Monks and Nuns). The other nine works are of less importance. For the study of Theravāda philosophy the Suttapiṭaka is the most important source.

To the Abhidhammapiṭaka (Basket of Scholasticism) belong seven individual books, the oldest of which appears to date back to the third, the youngest to the first, century B.C. It contains codifications of the teaching and analyses all central terms into so-and-so-many sub-terms in the form of lists and charts. Vinaya- and Suttapiṭaka employ conventional language, the Abhidhammapiṭaka a 'scientific' and 'psychological' one (of the third century B.C.). It no longer speaks of 'things' but of their elements and would have described water as H_2O had it known this way of expression. Whether it represents the liberating knowledge demanded by the Buddha seems questionable, the more so as it re-admits under new names some of the views which Gotama had rejected.

Of the numerous extra-canonical Pāli works those worth

mentioning are the *Milindapañha* (first century A.D.), which deals in dialogue form with the doctrine of rebirth without a transmigrating soul; the systematical handbook *Visuddhimagga* (Path to Purity) by Buddhaghosa (fifth century); and the scholastic manual *Abhidhammatthasaṅgaha* (Summary of the Meaning of Scholasticism) by Anuruddha (about eleventh century).

The Teachings of the Theravāda

The philosophy of Buddhism sprang from one single motive: the shock caused by suffering in the world. The experience of suffering supplies the impulse to Buddhist thinking, the analysis of suffering and the quest for liberation from it constitute its contents. Investigations which are of no use for liberation are regarded as worthless: Gotama the Buddha was a pragmatist, not a metaphysician. The structure of the Buddhist system, its contents and its limits are thus pre-defined.

I. ALL EXISTENCE IS SUFFERING

In his first sermon, delivered in the year 528 B.C. before those five monks in the Deer Park of Isipatana (Sārnāth) near Benares, Gotama explains what he understands by suffering:

> This, monks, is the Noble Truth of Suffering (*dukkha*): Birth is suffering, old age is suffering, illness is suffering, death is suffering; grief, lamentation, pain, affliction and despair are suffering; to be united with what is unloved, to be separated from what is loved is suffering; not to obtain what is longed for is suffering; in short, the Five Groups of Grasping are suffering.
>
> (Mv I, 6, 19 Vin I p. 10 = S 56, 11, 5 V p. 421)

Being the result of philosophical considerations this sentence is more pregnant with meaning than it seems on first sight. Moreover, since all its terms are connected with ideas which go beyond the obvious word meaning, we have to regard in turn: first the phenomena of birth, old age, grief, etc., second the term 'suffering', and third the teaching of the Five Groups which according to Buddhist conviction compose the empirical personality.

(1) Birth, old age and death, grief and despair, separation from friends, the company of disliked ones, non-fulfilment of desires—all these attributes of existence are suffering. As long

as they are not exterminated life cannot be called really happy. But since they are inseparable from it, life must be considered as sorrowful.

Here one may object that although existence is not sheer pleasure, it nevertheless keeps sufficient joy in store for a more positive assessment. In fact the Buddha in no way denies pleasures and pleasant experiences. On the contrary, he views them as a fixed part of life which otherwise would not appear as enticing as it does (S 22, 60 III p. 69 f.). His criteria of judgement are much profounder: It is permanence which he makes the yardstick of true happiness. Everything joyful and dear ends in suffering because it is transitory. It is false happiness, for it has to be counterbalanced with sorrow and tears. When during a stay in Sāvatthi the donor of the 'Eastpark Monastery', the matron Visākhā, approached Gotama at an unseemly hour and with her hair and clothes wet (from the ritual bath) to tell him of the death of her beloved granddaughter, he consoled the wailing woman with these words:

> He who has a hundred dear (things), Visākhā, has a hundred sufferings; he who has ninety . . . , ten . . . , five . . . , two dear (things), has ninety . . . , ten . . . , five . . . , two sufferings. For him who has no dear (thing) there is no suffering. Those, I declare, are griefless, without passion (and) free from despair.
>
> Whatever manifold griefs, sorrows, and sufferings there are in the world: They arise in dependence on dear (things); they do not arise, when there is nothing dear. (Ud 8, 8 p. 92)

Every mental attachment to something pleasant leads to suffering. To be sure, lust (*kāma*) and suffering are essentially the same. As the liberated monk Eraka puts it:

> Sorrowful are lusts, not joyful;
> who asks for lusts is asking for suffering.
> He who no longer asks for lusts
> he does not ask for suffering. (Thag 93)

(2) In the term 'suffering' (*dukkha*) lies a further difficulty in understanding Gotama's 'truth of suffering'.

A definition (S 38, 14 IV p. 259) which came into existence after the Buddha's death classifies threefold: Suffering resulting from pain (*dukkha-dukkha*), suffering from change or impermanence (*vipariṇāma-dukkha*), and suffering arising out of the personality-components (*saṅkhāra-dukkha*), that is from the fact that one has to exist as an individual and as such is exposed and susceptible to a thousand evils. The second type of suffering—on account of their impermanence—also includes pleasant (*sukha*) things and emotions; the third type comprises among others those adversities which have not yet emerged, but which we fear on the strength of intellectual anticipation.

The threefold definition analyses suffering according to its causes, but does not really cover the full meaning of the term. If the Buddha's 'truth of suffering' is to be more than a platitude then suffering must be more than a mere collective name for the well-known afflictions of life. It needed no sage to bring home to the world that grief, misery, pain, etc. are 'suffering' in the popular acceptation of the word. As a matter of fact *dukkha* in Buddhism is a philosophical term. Whatever is subject to the cycle (*saṃsāra*) of becoming and passing, is suffering, in other words everything that is unliberated. Used as an adjective *dukkha* ('sorrowful') expresses that the object thus designated belongs to the sphere of non-deliverance, to *saṃsāra*. The sentence: 'Birth, death, etc. are *dukkha*' is not an analytic but a synthetic statement. Interpreted it means: All phenomena connected with life as birth, death, aversion and separation are of saṃsāric nature and hence ineradicable as long as man abides in non-liberation.

(3) When according to Buddhism all saṃsāric existence is suffering, it is obvious that the empirical person as the focal point of the experience of suffering cannot be assessed differently. Indeed the sentence: 'In short, the Five Groups of Grasping are suffering' refers to personality.

2. THE SUBJECT OF SUFFERING AND THE THREE MARKS

In Buddhism the question of what man is is always answered by the enumeration of the Five Groups of Grasping (*upādāna-Kkhanda*)[8]:

> And which, monks, are in brief the Five Groups of Grasping which are sorrowful?:
> The Group of Grasping 'body' (*rūpa*),
> the Group of Grasping 'sensation' (*vedanā*),
> the Group of Grasping 'perception' (*saññā*),
> the Group of Grasping 'mental phenomena' (*saṅkhāra*),
> the Group of Grasping 'consciousness' (*viññāna*).
> (M 141 III p. 250)

'Body' (lit. 'form') means the physical frame of man, the space filled by bones, muscles, flesh and skin (M 28 I p. 190). Other passages (e.g. S 12, 2, 12) define the body as the organism formed of the four elements earth, water, fire and air, whereby these elements are understood as substantial material and at the same time the insubstantial qualities of extension, cohesion, temperature and movement.

The remaining four non-physical groups or components of the person are collectively called 'name' (*nāma*).

'Sensations' are the sense-impressions, the contacts of the sense-organs with objects of the external world. When these have been picked up by the brain and become reflections in the head of the observer, they are called 'perceptions'. They produce in man reactions which the Buddha collectively labels 'mental phenomena': notions, ideals, longings, moods, etc. Their common characteristic is that they all aim at, and press for, materialisation. Hence the expression 'mental phenomena' also includes the meaning 'intention', namely the

[8] They are called Groups of 'Grasping' (*upādāna*) because every undelivered being grasps, that is appropriates, them at the moment of rebirth as his new personality. According to M 109 III p. 16 they are rooted in craving (*chanda*), for it is the hankering after the 'Groups' which after the death of an unliberated person gives rise to new Groups in a womb.

intention to convert these longings and notions into realities.

Lastly 'consciousness' as the fifth Group is the accumulative element which collects the mental phenomena and is influenced, even created, by them. It is repeatedly interpreted as sense-consciousness, that is consciousness of something, and as terminating in death. Nevertheless it forms the connecting link to the next rebirth existence. Younger texts identify it with 'mind' or 'thought' (*citta*), so that 'consciousness' is also a designation of active and deliberate brain-work.

A problem crops up: Do the Five Groups exhaust the personality, or is there something belonging to personality beyond the Groups? The Pāli books do not pose this question so precisely, and therefore answer it neither in the negative nor in the affirmative. One thing, however, is certain, that in Buddhism man is always analysed into the Five Groups and only into these, and that the mental identification with these Groups results for him in suffering.

Why are the Five Groups suffering?

For two reasons. Firstly, because their existence is inseparably connected with the phenomena of birth, illness, longing and antipathy, etc., which in themselves are already suffering. Secondly, they are transient. Asked by a monk whether any one of the Groups is permanent, the Buddha replies:

> There is, monk, no body whatsoever which is permanent, fixed, lasting, not subject to the law of decay (and) forever remaining the same.
>
> There is, monk, no sensation whatsoever . . . , no perception whatsoever . . . , no mental phenomenon whatsoever . . . , no consciousness whatsoever which is permanent, fixed, lasting, not subject to the law of decay (and) forever the same. (S 22, 97, 9–13 III p. 147)

The impermanence of the Five Groups, that is of the personality, as well as the temporariness of all things, forms a central theme in Buddhist literature.

From the fact of the impermanence of the Five Groups the Buddha draws two significant conclusions. The first one, already mentioned, is that nothing transient (*anicca*) can be true happiness and that any existence as an individual has, therefore, to be regarded as sorrowful or suffering (*dukkha*). The second conclusion derives from the transitoriness of the Groups, that there is nothing in man which survives death. When all the Five Groups are subject to decay none of them can be a Self, an Ego, a Soul, for according to Indian convictions a soul is imperishable, unchanging and in essence free from suffering. The person or personality is non-self (*anatta*), merely an *empirical* person, nothing essential.

> What do you think, monks, is the body permanent or impermanent?
> Impermanent, Sir.
> Are the sensations . . . , perceptions . . . , mental phenomena . . . , is consciousness, permanent or impermanent?
> Impermanent, Sir.
> That which is impermanent, is it sorrowful or joyful?
> Sorrowful, Sir.
> Is it right then to regard that which is impermanent, sorrowful, subject to the law of decay, as 'This is mine, this am I, this is my Self'?
> Surely not, Sir. (M 22 I p. 138)

Impermanence, sorrowfulness and non-selfness—these are the Three Marks of the individual. The same features are, of course, also found in all inanimate things.

That no Self, no lasting Soul can be found in the Five Groups, i.e. the personality, is a fact not easily adopted by the average person, who sentimentally believes in the continuity of his Ego, and therefore needs proof. Gotama's first proof establishes non-selfness by pointing out the existence of qualities which are irreconcilable with a Self:

> The body, monks, is not a Self. For if, monks, this body were a Self, (then) this body would not tend to illness and one could achieve with regard to the body: 'Thus be my body!', 'Thus be my body not!' (S 22, 59, 3–4 III p. 66)

The same is said of the other Groups.

Only the first part of the sentence which deduces the non-selfness of the body etc. from its susceptibility, is logically correct. The second part contains false inference, for if the Five Groups were subject to the will, this would not be proof for, but against, their selfhood. A Self which can be influenced is looked upon as inconceivable in India.

The second proof operates with reference to the origination of the Groups:

> The body, monks, is not a Self. That which is the cause, the precondition to the origination of the body, that too is without a Self. How, monks, could the body, originating out of something which is not a Self, be a Self?
>
> (S 22, 20, 3–7 III p. 24)

Analogous statements follow for the other four Groups.

No use is made in this passage of the strongest argument: that the Five Groups cannot be a Self for the simple reason that they do arise, whereas a Self cannot originate as it is by definition timeless and eternal.

Sutta 28 of the *Majjhimanikāya* (I p. 185 ff.) contains an additional proof of the non-selfness of the body. It analyses the body into the Four Great Elements, viz. earth, water, fire and air, and declares these identical with the elements of nature. From this it follows that the body is but a part of the physical world, subject to change and consequently without selfhood.

As the doctrine of the Five Groups explains the person as a combination of soulless factors, an analogous teaching explains perception as a process which does not presuppose a Self as the subject of cognition. The monk Moliya-Phagguna, who enquired about the perceiving subject with the words 'Who exercises contact? Who senses?', got the following reply from the Buddha:

> This question is not permissible . . . I do not say: '*He* exercises contact'. Were I to speak (like that) the appropriate question would be: '*Who* exercises contact, Sir?' (But) I do

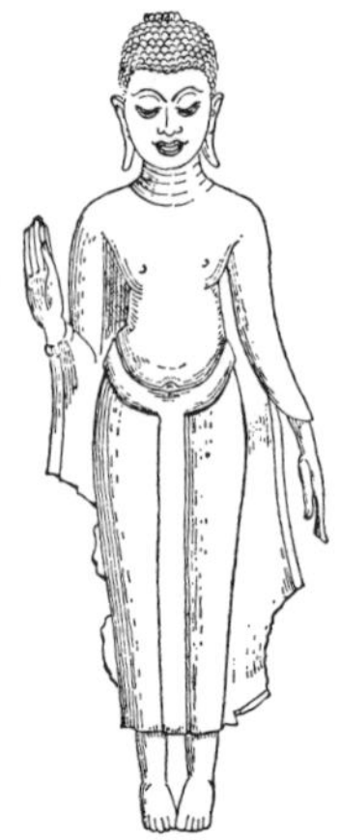

The Buddha in the gesture of granting consolation and appeasement of passions. (After a Thai bronze of uncertain date, perhaps 15th century.)

not speak thus. However, were I, who do not say this, asked: 'From what precondition, Sir, (arises) contact?', (then) this question would be permissible. The correct answer here is: 'From the Sixfold Sphere of (sense-) Contact as precondition (arises sense-) contact; from (sense-) contact as precondition (arises) sensation. (S 12, 12, 4 II p. 13)

The acts of perception behind which unphilosophical thought supposes a soul as subject of cognition are in Buddhism dissolved into a series of impersonal processes. One ought not to think: 'I perceive', but: 'A process of perception is taking place in the Five Groups'. To deduce from the process of cognition the existence of a Soul, is a fallacy.

To gain insight into the transitoriness, sorrowfulness and non-selfness of the personality composed of the Five Groups would be easier could one assume an impartial attitude toward oneself. This, however, is difficult since much ephemeral joy is connected with the Groups, which camouflages the fundamental unpleasantness of all saṃsāric existence. But when the conviction of non-selfness has taken root in a person, it leads him to equanimity and superior composure. Only things with which a man identifies himself are able to disturb his mind—

only that which concerns 'myself' can give 'me' grief. If the Five Groups, which one calls 'my' personaliity, are not in reality a Self, then no misery that befalls them concerns 'me'. This attitude, of course, does not allay pain but it helps one to bear and mentally to overcome it. Buddhism is convinced that it is not the circumstances in which a person finds himself that determine his well-being, but his mastery over them.

Gotama's axiom that the empirical person neither is nor contains a Self has made some Western Buddhists assume that he advocated a Self or Soul outside the Five Groups: If the Soul is not within the Groups then it must be somewhere else, that is transcendent. This view is the result of speculations[9] which would not meet with Gotama's approval. He inculcated on his followers that the Five Groups possess no selfhood; he did not say more on this subject.

Suggestive of his attitude towards this problem is a passage in the *Saṃyuttanikāya* (44, 10, 3 ff. IV p. 400 f.), where the itinerant ascetic Vacchagotta asks him whether there is a Self or not. The Buddha refuses to answer. Since in India a Self is always conceived as something eternal, a reply in the affirmative would have meant that there is no possibility for the extinction of individuality in the state of liberation. On the other hand, a reply in the negative would have led the questioner to surmise that there is no rebirth. Both alternatives contradict the Buddhist teaching and neither of the two answers would have made the questioner understand that the empirical person is only a bundle of phenomena without something lasting as an essence.

To the Buddha the question of a Self was insignificant. His thinking did not operate in terms of being and substance but in those of processes of becoming and conditional dependencies. Not even the doctrine of rebirth postulates a Self, as will be shown in the following section.

[9] And of biased translations. The Pāli language employs nomina without a definite and indefinite article. Those who translate: 'The body is not *the* Self' (instead of neutrally: '. . . *a* Self') presuppose the existence of a Self, but have not proved it by the text. *Attan* is moreover the reflexive pronoun.

3. (EXCURSUS): OBJECTIVE AND SUBJECTIVE EXISTENCE

Early Buddhism regards the world as real and understands it to be identical with its phenomena. When these disappear, the world, too, ceases to exist. A 'thing in itself' behind the appearances or an Absolute is denied.

However, it makes a clear distinction between the objective and subjective reality of the world. Man through his birth is cast into the objective world, which provides the basis for his physical existence. But only after he has grasped it with his sense-organs and perceived it does the world become a mental and so subjective reality for him:

> What, monks, is the Universe?: The eye and forms, the ear and sounds, the nose and smells, the tongue and tastes, the body and tactile objects, the mind and mental objects. (S 35, 23, 3 IV p. 15)

As the text makes clear, not five but six organs of perception appertain to man's bodily equipment; namely, besides eye, ear, nose, tongue and tactile sense, there is the mind (*manas*) as the organ of thinking. It is the tool for the production of ideas, the cognition of non-material facts, and for comprehending the relationships between things, conceptions, ideals and/or recollections. The facts so obtained by the mind then constitute the contents of thought, namely mental objects (*dhamma*).

Three factors, so the Buddha goes on, must be present for the world to be realised: the above-mentioned six organs of perception, the sense-objects corresponding to them and the respective sense-consciousness (*viññāna*), that is awareness of the objects. In the union of these three lies the (subjective) origin of the world (S 12, 44, 3–9 II p. 73). The *Majjhimanikāya* outlines this theory more explicitly:

> When . . . an eye and forms (= visible objects) are there then consciousness of sight arises. The meeting of (these) three (factors) is contact; from the precondition of contact

> (arises) sensation; that which is sensed is perceived; that which is perceived is thought over; that which is thought over is projected (*papañceti*) (as the external world) . . .
> (M 18 I p. 111 f.)

The same holds true for the other sense-organs.

The passage thus says that we do not apprehend the world as it is but as we imagine it to be according to the impressions we receive from our senses. Whether the sense-organs supply a correct picture of the world is not examined, as it is not the world which is the subject of Buddhist analysis but the being suffering in it.

That the world with its suffering becomes a personal reality only when reflected in the mirror of consciousness is a knowledge which already contains the key to deliverance. It allows one to infer that the termination of suffering, in so far as it arises from contacts with the world, can be realised by and within man. This is the sense of the Buddha's words to Rohitassa:

> I declare, friend, that in this fathom-long body with its perception and thinking (lies) the world, the origin of the world, the cessation of the world and the way to the cessation of the world. (A 4, 45, 3 II p. 48)

The theory proceeds yet one step further. For in his mind man creates not only his world, but also himself. Only he lives, who reflects his own existence in consciousness. When consciousness dwindles away then also 'name and body' (*nāma-rūpa*),[10] that is the Five Groups (*khandha*) are subjectively done away with:

[10] *Nāma-rūpa* is a collective term for the Five Groups which compose the empirical personality. *Rūpa* designates the physical organism, *nāma* the mental-psychical processes taking place in it. S 12, 2, 12 II p. 3 f. defines: Sensation, perception, intention, contact, deliberation—this is called 'name'. The Four Great Elements (earth, water, fire, air) and the form dependent on (them) . . . , that is called 'body'.

> Consciousness is peerless, endless (and) radiating all round; here neither water (and) earth (nor) fire and air have a hold; long and short, fine and coarse, beautiful and ugly, 'Name and Form'—all this is completely annulled: Through the destruction of consciousness (all) this here will come to an end. (D 11, 85 I p. 223)

4. THE CYCLE OF REBIRTH

In Buddhist evaluation one life is already suffering enough; how much more the multitude of existences which every being has to pass through. For with death, so the Buddha proclaims, existence is by no means at an end. The death of an unliberated person is necessarily followed by his rebirth, in which the suffering of living and dying is repeated. To be born and to die and be born again—this is the cycle of *saṃsāra*.

The primordial beginning of this cycle is outside Gotama's interest as any speculation about it cannot contribute to liberation. Beginningless, he teaches, is the chain of previous existences and it is depressing to look back at the saṃsāric suffering endured by each being:

> Out of the beginningless, monks, comes the wandering (of beings in the cycle of rebirths). No first point can be seen from which the(se) beings, caught in ignorance (*avijjā*), bound by craving (*taṅhā*), rove and wander (in *saṃsāra*).
>
> What, monks, do you think is more: the water in the Four Great Oceans or the tears, which you have shed when roving, wandering, lamenting and weeping while on this long way, because you received what you hated and did not receive what you loved? (S 15, 1, 7 II p. 179)

Oppressive, too, is the glance into the future. New deaths, new births, new suffering—these are the prospects. Yet Gotama's Dhamma is no pessimism. As he teaches the possibility of liberation from suffering, it distinctly bears an optimistic character.

5. THE DOCTRINE OF KAMMA

The statement that rebirth is unavoidable for the unliberated one does not imply that the new form of existence must necessarily be a human one. Quite on the contrary, a human form of existence is considered difficult to obtain and rare. Buddhist cosmography lists five, sometimes six, realms into which a person can be reborn: the sphere of the gods, the world of man, the sphere of spirits (*peta*), that of animals, and hell (M 12 I p. 73 ff.). Some texts also speak of a realm of demons (*asura*).

Though the life-span of beings in the various realms is very different—no being escapes death. Existence in hell, too, is not for an unlimited period, for no deed can be so vile as to result in eternal punishment. It is the same in the heavenly sphere. Gods live longer and in happier circumstances than humans, but like all other beings have to step down as soon as the good deeds on account of which they became gods have worn out. Even Brahman (Sahampati), in early Buddhist times the highest god of the Indian pantheon, is subject to the universal cycle of becoming and destruction (A 10, 29, 2 V p. 60) and not exempt from death and rebirth.

An existence in a human embodiment is certainly not the highest, but in Buddhist opinion is the most favourable one for liberation. The beings in hell, animals, spirits and demons are too dull, the gods in their blissfulness too haughty to see the necessity for liberation. Only when reborn as human beings are they capable of grasping the teaching of the Buddha and of following the way to emancipation. Moreover, admission into the Buddhist monastic order is open only to man. A human embodiment therefore is preferable to all other forms of existence.

The form in which a being is reborn after death is not in the least a matter of accident. The law of causation governs here as it does in the physical world where every effect has its cause and corresponds with that cause. Applied to the sphere of ethics and rebirth, Indian philosophy calls this law '*kamma*': Favourable rebirth is caused by good deeds (*kamma*), unfavourable rebirth by bad deeds. Buddhism does not know of 'sin', i.e. offence against the commandments of god or a god. It only distinguishes between wholesome (*kusala* or *puñña*) and unwholesome (*akusala* or *apuñña*) deeds—those leading towards liberation and those leading away from it. The balance between the wholesome and the unwholesome actions of a being at the close of his life determine the kind and quality of his next existences. Being asked why some beings are born into unpleasant, others into pleasant, embodiment, the master replies:

> Because of their wicked conduct, their unjust conduct... some beings with the break up of the body, after death... go the bad way, come to places of pain, to hell... Owing to their conduct in agreement with the teaching, their considerate conduct, some beings with the break up of the body, after death, go the good way, come to the heavenly world. (A 2, 2, 6 I p. 55 f.)
>
> Deed divides beings into lower and higher ones. (M 135 III p. 203)

Our present existence is the result of deeds performed by ourselves in previous existences. The body is an 'old deed' (S 12, 37, 3 II p. 65), and to suffer means to endure kammic effects, that is to lie on the bed one has made. Our future forms of existence are determined by our actions of today; we are now laying the foundations of our future 'fate'. *Kamma* in the view of the Hīnayāna is a neutral natural law that admits no exception or interference, but of which, by acting accordingly, man can avail himself in order to obtain the rebirth wished for. No need to mention that even the happiest rebirth is not yet liberation.

It would be quite wrong to interpret the doctrine of kamma along deterministic lines. Only the quality, that is the social surrounding, the physical appearance and the mental abilities of a person are fixed by the deeds of his previous existences,

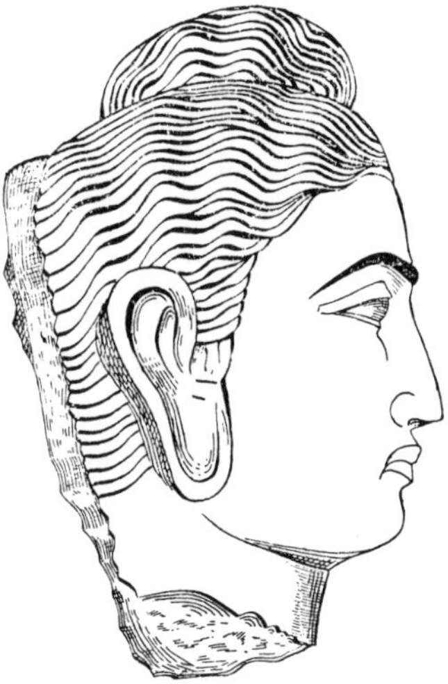

The Buddha, Gandhāra style (after a sculpture of the 2nd–4th century). The features and the wavy hair suggest the hellenistic origin of Gandhāra art. The Greek hair knot was adopted into Indian art and by native iconographers later interpreted as a protuberance of the skull (*uṣṇīṣa*).

but in no way his actions. Without cognising free will as a philosophical problem, Gotama takes it for granted that the innate character of each being leaves him the freedom to decide about the actions which determine his future.

Wholesome deeds help man to achieve better rebirth and thus bring him nearer to salvation; they do not, however, lead straight to liberation, to riddance of all rebirth. Deeds are something finite and cannot bear fruit beyond the finite. Even the best obtainable form of existence still lies within the cycle of rebirths. Nevertheless, Gotama does not disapprove of action in general:

> I teach action . . . as well as non-action . . . I teach the non-performance of bad deeds with body . . . speech and thought, of the many bad, unwholesome things . . . I teach the performance of good deeds with body . . . speech and thought, of the many wholesome things. (A 2, 4, 3 I p. 62)

But if wholesome actions entangle man as much in *saṃsāra* as unwholesome deeds, how should one act? Is it advisable, is it at all possible, to abstain from all action?

The Buddha's answer is a psychological one. It is not the action in itself, he explains, which determines the kammic future, but its motive, the mental attitude preceding it: Not the execution of the action but the action-intention (*saṅkhāra* or *cetanā*) shapes the future existence. Supposing somebody is prevented from executing an intended action by outer circumstances: The bare action-intention suffices to produce the corresponding kammic effect. Only those deeds are free from kammic results which the seeker for liberation performs without greed, hatred and delusion.

> Whatever deed, monks, has been performed without greed, without hatred and free from delusion . . . after greed, hatred (and) delusion were done away with—this deed is annihilated, cut off at the root, made similar to a rooted-out palm tree, prevented from becoming (i.e. kammic ripening), in future not subject to the law of becoming.
>
> (A 3, 33, 2 I p. 135)

This is the Buddhist way to liberation: to act but without greed for success, free from the wish to harm anybody and with reason. If there were no possibility of performing good deeds without becoming bound by kamma, the enchainment of man with *saṃsāra* would be indissoluble, and he would have no chance of ever escaping from suffering.

The fact that the rebirth-existence is determined more by the mental attitude of the doer than by the actual deed furthermore entails that the same deed may yield different effects with different persons. An action which influences an ethically unstable person for a long time in a negative way may in the case of an ethically sound person be confined to minimal effects. A lump of salt in a cup makes its contents undrinkable, the same amount of salt in the river Ganges leaves the water as it was. (A 3, 99 I p. 249 ff.)

Besides actions resulting in rebirth, Buddhism distinguishes those which already bear kammic fruits in this life. It is even considered an advantage when a bad deed is redeemed in the present existence. A typical example is the case of the robber Aṅgulimāla. After having realised the depravity of his conduct and having donned the robe of a monk, one day he was pelted with stones during his alms round. When the Buddha saw him bleeding and with his robe torn, he remarked:

> Endure it, brahmin! The ripening of a deed (*kamma*) for which you could boil many years . . . in hell, the ripening of this deed you now experience in your lifetime.
>
> (M 86 II p. 104)

6. THE CAUSE OF REBIRTH

The Buddha pronounces on the force propelling the cycle of rebirth in his 'Truth of the Origin of Suffering':

> This, monks, is the Noble Truth of the Origin of Suffering: it is craving (*taṇhā*) that leads to rebirth, is pleasurable, connected with passion (and) takes delight here and there, namely: craving for lust, craving for becoming, craving for destruction. (Mv 1, 6, 20 Vin I p. 10 = S 56, 11, 6 V p. 421)

Craving—in Buddhist books sometimes rendered as 'thirst' or 'desire'—binds beings to *saṃsāra* and drives them from life to life:

> I do not see, monks, any other fetter being bound by which the beings rush through, hurry through the long night (of incessant rebirths), than . . . the fetter of craving. (Itiv 15)

Craving, the I- and mine-egoism, is closely connected with the erroneous belief in a Self, a Soul.

The 'Truth of the Origin of Suffering' distinguishes between three kinds of craving: craving for lust, for becoming and for destruction. The most vital of them is craving for lust (*kāma*) particularly since it also includes sexual desire and the wish to enjoy and possess. Irrespective of whether it finds fulfilment or not, it results in suffering. In the case of non-fulfilment man behaves like a little boy who cries as he cannot have the silvery moon to play with. The moon does not cause him grief, but his covetousness. If, however, craving finds satisfaction, the feeling of happiness is but short-lived. Even if the object obtained does not immediately reveal itself as disappointing, its possession soon becomes a habit and more is desired and it is transient and leads to the suffering caused by loss. Suffering is inherent in all craving.

Craving to become means for new forms of existence. It produces suffering as it binds one to the cycle of rebirth, from which a wiser man would try to escape. When craving has as its object a life free from suffering, it aims at something impossible, inasmuch as all rebirth is transient and sorrowful.

Craving for destruction is the desire that something unpleasant may not come to pass—an attitude by which the incident feared gains power over one's mind even before it becomes a reality. In its specific connotation craving for destruction is the reversal of craving for existence, namely the urge towards self-annihilation. Suicide, however, does not lead to liberation[11] as it destroys only the body but not the *kamma*; it merely causes a change in the form of existence. The unliberated suicide after rebirth will again encounter his old *kamma* until he has finally lived it down and exhausted its kammic effect. Liberation from the saṃsāric chain of rebirths is only possible through extinction, i.e. *nibbāna*. But *nibbāna* cannot be realised through craving: on the contrary it is the result of the annihilation of craving.

As with everything else in the world, craving too has a cause, namely sensual and mental contacts with objects. Pleasant sense-experiences and ideas produce craving for lust

[11] Except in the case of a saint who, after the annihilation of craving and ignorance which compel to rebirth, is not threatened by new becoming. His suicide is not motivated by craving for destruction, but is the result of wise reflection of reasons, such as incurable illness.

Head of a meditating Buddha, Khmer style, from Thailand. Date uncertain, perhaps 12th century.

and becoming, unpleasant ones craving for destruction. Hence it is understandable that the Buddha regards the guarding of the sense-gates as an important discipline for liberation.

That craving (*taṇhā*) alone keeps the cycle of births and deaths in motion was unquestionably Gotama's original conviction. He later complemented it by declaring that ignorance (*avijjā*) also partakes in this function. If it is enlightenment that liberates a person and converts him into a Buddha or saint, it is only logical to assume that the unliberated being is bound by his ignorance. In a narrower sense ignorance is understood as non-awareness of suffering (in Buddhist philosophical meaning) and nescience of the teaching of the Buddha; in a wider sense as spiritual blindness. Many Suttas place craving and ignorance side by side as causes of suffering and name them together.

Pāli books mention craving and ignorance as a pair as often as they speak of a triad of causes of suffering: greed (*lobha*), hatred (*dosa*) and delusion (*moha*). Hatred is the reverse of craving and delusion close in meaning to ignorance. Even if the triad were not a mere elaboration of the pair it is, on factual grounds, admissible to deem both formulas equivalent.

An apparently later usage refers to the causes of suffering

by the collective name of 'influences' (*āsava*) or 'defilements' (*kilesa*). The uprooting of the influences leads straight to liberation. (M 51 I p. 348)

7. CONDITIONED ORIGINATION

Difficulties in comprehending the Buddhist doctrine of rebirth arise mainly from Gotama's denial of a Self in the Five Groups. Without a Self, or Soul, which survives death and enters a new body, without transmigration, no rebirth can apparently take place, for *what* could then be reborn?

According to the Buddha's teaching rebirth indeed operates without a transmigrating soul. The continuity of the chain of rebirths does not lie in an imperishable substratum, but in the conditionism of the forms of existence: each rebirth conditions another. Even though the simile is halting, one can illustrate this process with billiard-balls. Tapping a ball makes it roll for some distance and set the next ball in motion. This ball in its turn transmits the impulse to the third one. Nothing material passes over from the first ball to the second and third, but each ball by its impact gives the next one motion and a certain, by no means accidental, direction. In Buddhism thinking in terms of substances is replaced by thought in terms of conditionalities. In the Nexus of Conditioned Origination (*paticcasamuppāda*) the texts furnish the theoretical foundation for this kind of thinking.

The Pāli canon knows several forms of the Nexus which differ from one another in the number of their links. So far as their contents are concerned they all run parallel but only the complete chain with twelve links can be the object of analysis:

From the precondition (1) *ignorance* (arise) action-intentions;
from the precondition (2) *action-intentions* (arises) consciousness;
from the precondition (3) *consciousness:* name and body;
from the precondition (4) *name and body:* the sixfold sphere of sense-contact;
from the precondition (5) *the sixfold sphere of sense-contact:* contact;

from the precondition (6) *contact:* sensation;
from the precondition (7) *sensation:* craving;
from the precondition (8) *craving:* grasping;
from the precondition (9) *grasping:* becoming;
from the precondition (10) *becoming:* birth;
from the precondition (11) *birth*
arise (12) *old age* and *death*, *grief*, *lamentation*, *pain*, *affliction* and *despair*. This is the origin of the whole mass of suffering. (M 38 I p. 261).

The Pāli name of this formula—*paṭiccasamuppāda*, 'conditioned origination'—indicates how one should understand the relation between the links of the Nexus. It is no causal dependence as *causa* is the technical term for a cause which alone, without any assisting factor, produces an effect. The dependence of the links is rather a 'conditionism', for each link is a *conditio*, that is one condition beside others for the succeeding link's coming into being.

The Nexus of Conditioned Origination is easier to comprehend if placed parallel to the series of the Five Groups (*khandha*) —body, sensation, perception, mental phenomena and consciousness—which combined constitute the empirical person. Some of the links appear in both the series which are said to form chains of conditioned factors. But how can it be explained that the two series list identical links in different orders of succession: that the Five-Group-series places '*saṅkhāras*' and 'consciousness' after, but the Nexus before, 'body'?

The answer is contained in the purposes of both chains. The Five Groups list the constituents of the person; the Nexus of Conditioned Origination on the other hand is meant to elucidate the sequence of rebirths which exceeds the single person. As its twelve links cover three rebirth existences it includes the series of the Five Groups three times.[12]

[12] The classical Buddhist exegesis also regards the Nexus as covering three existences, e.g. Vism 17 II p. 578 and Ak 3, 20 p. 57. Both texts divide it into 2+8+2 links. This unconvincing model is departed from in the following table.

In the following table the two chains are combined in such a way as to place the links common to both of them side by side and the others according to their conditionality one under the other.

The Five Groups	*The Nexus of Conditioned Origination*	
1. Body		First Existence
2. Sensation		
3. Perception		
	1. Ignorance	
4. Saṅkhāras[13]	2. Saṅkhāras	
5. Consciousness	3. Consciousness	
1. Body	4. Name and body	Second Existence
	5. Sixfold sphere of sense contacts	
	6. Contact	
2. Sensation	7. Sensation	
3. Perception		
4. Saṅkhāras		
5. Consciousness		
	8. Craving	
	9. Grasping	
	10. Becoming	Third Existence
1. Body		
	11. Birth	
2. Sensation		
3. Perception		
4. Saṅkhāras		
5. Consciousness		
	12. Old Age and Death	

This juxtaposition exposes two weaknesses of the Nexus: 1. Why is it that each one of the three rebirth-existences is outlined in different words? 2. Why does the First Existence only mention *ignorance* and the Second only *craving* as cause of

[13] The Pāli expression is here retained as it would otherwise have to be rendered differently in each chain. Within the Five Groups '*saṅkhāra*' designates mental phenomena (above, p. 42); in the Nexus of Conditioned Origination: action-intentions. Nevertheless the terms are so closely cognate that they may be identified here.

the succeeding rebirth? For the cause of rebirth must always be the same: *either* ignorance *or* craving *or* both of them together.

Only a historical inspection can answer these questions. The Nexus of Conditioned Origination came about through the linking of three originally separate conditional chains (probably consisting of links 1 to 4; 4 to 8; and 8 to 12), which Gotama during his long teaching career had used in his sermons. Obviously the early monks believed that in combining them and thereby forming the Nexus of Conditioned Origination they had made a great step forward. Otherwise they would not have devoted so much space to the Nexus in the canon nor ventured to attribute it to the master.

8. THE NEXUS OF CONDITIONED ORIGINATION IN DETAIL

IGNORANCE (*avijjā*), with which the formula commences, is in the Pāli sources defined in the following way:

> Not-knowing of suffering, the origin of suffering, the termination of suffering (and) the way leading to the termination of suffering—this . . . is called ignorance. (M 9 I p. 54)

According to this, ignorance is not understood as lack of knowledge but specifically as non-acquaintance with the Four Noble Truths into which the Buddha arranges his teaching. He who is unfamiliar with the teaching and, abiding in spiritual blindness, does not recognise the general suffering of all saṃsāric existence—he from his ignorance develops saṅkhāras. And these decide the type of his next rebirth.

'SAṄKHĀRA' has several meanings in the Buddhist scriptures. In the Nexus of Conditioned Origination as in the doctrine of kamma it signifies intentions (*cetanā*), especially the action-intentions which precede the execution of the action. Since actions or deeds can be bodily, linguistic and mental, a distinction is made between intentions of the body, of language, and of thought. (S 12, 2, 14 II p. 4)

The action-intentions—more than the actual action—are decisive for rebirth:

> I will show you, monks, rebirth according to the action-intentions . . . There is . . . a monk endowed with faithful confidence (*saddhā*) . . . To him (the thought) occurs: 'Oh, if I could only be reborn after the disintegration of my body, after death, into a community of wealthy warriors!' He maintains this thought, he adheres to this thought, he cultivates this thought. His action-intentions and his dwelling (on them) will lead him to rebirth there (in that community).
> (M 120 III p. 99 f.)

This passage points out that the action-intentions not only effect rebirth, but also determine its kind and quality.

How they do this is explained in all detail in the Pāli sources. Action-intentions can be of three qualities: good, bad, and neutral. The quality of the CONSCIOUSNESS (*viññāna*) which arises in dependence on action-intentions tallies exactly with the quality of the latter:

> When, monks, an ignorant person produces a good action-intention (*saṅkhāra*), his consciousness (*viññāna*) is bent towards the good. When he produces a bad action-intention, . . . a neutral action-intention, his consciousness is bent towards the bad, . . . towards the neutral. (S 12, 51, 12 II p. 82)

After the death of a being his good, bad or neutral consciousness descends into a correspondingly good, bad or neutral womb and occasions in it the origin of NAME AND BODY (*nāma-rūpa*), that is a new (good, bad or neutral) empirical person:

> From the precondition consciousness (arise) Name and Body, thus have I declared. This . . . is to be understood thus . . .: If . . . the consciousness (of a deceased being) did not descend into a mother's womb, could Name and Body then

arise in this womb?—Surely not, Sir! (replies the questioned monk). (D 15, 21 II p. 62 f.)

The consciousness of the deceased enters the womb of a future mother; it does not enter the empirical 'person' which originates in this womb as a rebirth. Consciousness, therefore, is not a Soul or Self (*attan*) which changes over into a new form of existence. It acts like a catalyst which triggers off a chemical process, but is no longer present in its final product.

In the *Majjhimanikāya* (38 I p. 258) Gotama emphatically rejects the view that consciousness is a permanent entity which migrates through the chain of rebirths. The correct opinion is: 'This consciousness turns back (*paccudāvattati*), (in the Nexus) it does not go beyond 'Name and Body' (D 14, 2, 19 II p. 32). The reborn person develops his own consciousness which is not identical with that of his previous existence.

Again: Into which womb the consciousness descends depends on the latter's kammic tendency. A consciousness which sprang up from good action-intentions, and so is of good quality, will after the death of its present 'owner' seek a correspondingly good womb with favourable hereditary dispositions. Provided that the biological conditions are fulfilled,[14] it induces in this womb the development of a new being without itself changing over into it. After the birth of the new being the quality of his existence is in exact accordance with the quality of the action-intentions which were the kammic cause of his origination. The doctrine of *kamma* has thus been given a detailed working description.

Links 5 to 12 of the Nexus of Conditioned Origination are not all that difficult to understand. The term SIXFOLD SPHERE OF SENSE-CONTACTS (*saḷāyatana*) refers to the fields of objects presenting themselves to the six senses—sight, hearing, smell, taste, touch and thought—of the new being

[14] M 38 I p. 256 and M 93 II p. 157 point out that besides the consciousness searching for a womb—the 'germ' (*gabbha*) or 'spirit' (*gandhabba*)—parental procreation and the mother's readiness for conception are necessary for a new being to come about.

after birth. Between the sixfold sense-spheres, that is the object-world, and the sense-organs CONTACTS (*phassa*) take place and occasion SENSATIONS (*vedanā*) which soon mature to CRAVING (*taṇhā*). Craving again leads the consciousness of the being after his death to renewed GRASPING (*upādāna*) of a womb. Here the consciousness causes the BECOMING (*bhava*) of a new being which results in BIRTH (*jāti*) into a sorrowful existence. The end is again OLD AGE and DEATH (*jarā-maraṇa*).

9. CONDITIONED ORIGINATION AS THE FOUNDATION OF INDIVIDUAL EXISTENCE

In the Pāli canon a monk raises the question for the bearer of this conditional happening: To whom belong, and for whom occur, the phenomena mentioned in the Nexus of Conditioned Origination? The Buddha replies:

> (This) question is not permissible . . . If a monk would say: 'What are the (phenomena mentioned in the Nexus) . . . and to whom do they belong . . .?', (the reply should be:) 'Both these are one, only differing as expressions' . . . The Perfect One preaches the true teaching (as lying) in the middle: From (the link preceding in the Nexus) . . . as its precondition arises (the succeeding link) . . .
>
> (S 12, 35, 3 ff. II p. 61 ff.)

The Nexus has no 'bearer', and is not supported by a substance, but from the sequence of its short-lived factors forms itself the empirical individual and his chain of rebirths. Existence is a process of fluctuation, not being. Just as arranged sounds make up a melody, so do conditional ephemeral phenomena constitute the chain of existences. Nexus of Conditioned Origination = empirical person = suffering—this is the formula which underlies the Buddhist conception of man.

Closely connected with this image of the individual is the problem of the identity between the beings of a succession of rebirths. The unclothed ascetic Kassapa enquired of the Buddha

Bodh-Gayā is sacred not only to Buddhists but also to Hindus. In the 8th century the Hindus declared the Buddha the Ninth Incarnation of the God Visnu. The Mahābodhi temple and the Bodhi tree are today under joint Hindu-Buddhist administration. Harmoniously Hindus and Buddhists meet under the descendant of the Bodhi tree to honour the great teacher.

Sārnāth (Isipatana) near Benares, the place of the first sermon of the Buddha and of the foundation of the monastic order. The Dhamekh *stūpa* in its present shape (height: 44 m) was completed between the 4th and the 6th century A.D. and contains as nucleus a small brick *stūpa* of the Asoka period. It marks the place of Gotama's sermon to the five ascetics who then became his first followers. A second Asoka *stūpa* which in later times was several times encased was in 1794 demolished for the sake of plundering the bricks; the relics of the Buddha found in it were submerged in the Ganges.
Of the Mūlagandhakūṭī temple, originally 60 m in height, which marks the spot of the Buddha's meditation and was described by Hsuan-tsang in the 7th century, only the foundation-walls remain. The same is true of seven monasteries the oldest of which dates from the 2nd century B.C., the youngest from the 12th century. From the 13th century onwards Sārnāth fell into decay.

whether according to his teaching it is the same or a different person who suffers the consequences of previous deeds (*kamma*) in the form of a rebirth. Gotama replies:

> By saying: 'He acts, he (himself) enjoys (the fruit of his action)', . . . one arrives at (the evaluation of man) as eternal. By saying: 'One acts, another enjoys (the fruit of the action)', . . . one arrives at (the evaluation of man) as destructible. Not falling for either extreme the Perfect One showed the teaching (as lying) in the middle: From ignorance as precondition (arise) action-intentions . . . (etc.). (S 12, 17, 14 ff. II p. 20)

Since there is no immortal Self which runs through the various lives like a silk thread through a string of pearls, it cannot be the same person who reaps the fruit of kammic seeds of past existences in rebirth. On the other hand the reborn person is not completely different, for each form of existence is caused by, and proceeds from, its previous existence like a flame which is lit by another one. The truth lies in between identity and isolation: In conditional dependence.

Despite the lack of a substratum between the beings in a chain of rebirths it is considered possible to remember one's pre-existences, though of course only at a high level of perfection. Describing his enlightenment-experience Gotama says:

> I remembered many previous existences, namely one birth, two . . . , three . . . , four . . . , five . . . , ten . . . , twenty . . . , fifty . . . , hundred births: . . . There I was, had that name, belonged to that family, that was my caste, that my livelihood, I have experienced such happiness and sorrow, that was my end; deceased I came again into existence there: there I was, had that name . . . (M 36 I p. 248)

10. THE TERMINATION OF SUFFERING

Since according to the 'Truth of the Origin of Suffering' craving (*taṇhā*) is the cause of suffering, the termination of suffering is possible through annihilation of craving:

Gotama expounding the doctrine. The right hand which is raised with its palm facing outwards does not withhold any knowledge which could be conducive to deliverance. The left hand rests in the gesture of meditation. (Tibetan wood-cut.)

> This, monks, is the Noble Truth of the termination of suffering; the complete extinction, destruction, abandonment, rejection, leaving (and) casting off of this very craving.
> (Mv 1, 6, 21 Vin I p. 10 = S 56, 11, 7 V p. 421)

With the extirpation of craving the sorrowful cycle of rebirth finds an end for that respective being.

Other texts name ignorance (*avijjā*) besides craving as the cause of samsāric suffering, meaning thereby nescience of the Four Noble Truths of Buddhism. So it is said:

> Those who again and again enter
> the cycle of birth and death:
> From this existence to the next
> they enter by their ignorance. (Snip 729)

Consequently ignorance, too, is to be rooted out if liberation is sought. The goal can never be reached without enlightenment (*bodhi*), that is without realising the sorrowfulness of all existence and without apprehending the possibility of the annihilation of suffering.

How does the destruction of craving and ignorance effect deliverance?

By terminating the *kamma* process. According to the doctrine of *Kamma* all actions bring on consequences which qualitatively correspond with them, except those which are performed free from greed, hatred and delusion, in other words: without craving and ignorance. He who is no longer bound to the circle of rebirths by his actions or action-intentions is close to extinction (*nibbāna*).

II. THE EIGHTFOLD WAY TO THE TERMINATION OF SUFFERING

To assume that in their present life more than a few advanced seekers are able to conquer craving and ignorance would be to overrate man. Most men will need a long time, a whole series of rebirths in which by good deeds they gradually work themselves upwards to better forms of existence. Finally, however, everyone will obtain an embodiment of such great ethical possibilities that he can destroy craving and ignorance in himself and escape the compulsion for further rebirth. It is regarded as certain that all who strive for emancipation will gain it sometime or other.

The Buddha did not speak about the highest goal to every audience in order not to discourage people from the very beginning. He used to remind non-Buddhists and the simpler among his lay followers of their duties towards family and society and urge them to do good works of which the kammic effect is rebirth in heaven. However, he made it plain to the more intelligent laymen and to monks that heavenly rebirth is but a temporary goal as it still lies within the realm of *saṃsāra*. The final goal should be deliverance from *saṃsāra*: *Nibbāna*, which can only be reached by eradicating the causes of suffering, namely craving and ignorance.

Gotama's Fourth Truth states how total freedom from suffering can be achieved. As it is necessary to extirpate both craving and ignorance, it contains rules for self-discipline which are conducive to the annihilation of craving, and also an intellectual demand for Right View (= termination of ignorance).

> This, monks, is the Noble Truth of the Way to the Termination of Suffering, namely:
> (1) Right View,
> (2) Right Resolve,
> (3) Right Speech,
> (4) Right Conduct,
> (5) Right Livelihood,
> (6) Right Effort,
> (7) Right Awareness,
> (8) Right Meditation.
>
> (Mv 1, 6, 22 Vin I p. 10 = S 56, 11, 8 V p. 421)

These rules are not sections of a way which the seeker has to cover one by one but virtues to be developed simultaneously. The interrelation existing between them makes it impossible to neglect one rule without impeding the realisation of the others.

Some texts divide the Eightfold Way into three groups, namely:

wisdom (*paññā*)	—members 1 and 2
morality (*sīla*)	—members 3 to 5, and
meditation (*samādhi*)	—members 6 to 8.

As with the Eightfold Way this threefold division should not be viewed as a sequence of stages. Otherwise it would also contradict other statements in the Pāli sources which represent wisdom as the highest virtue immediately preceding liberation.

Here are the rules of the Eightfold Way in detail.

(1) Right View (*sammā-diṭṭhi*) is the knowledge of the Buddhist Four Truths (D 22, 21 II p. 312) and the recognition that 'a Self is not mine (and) what originates . . . (and) perishes

is but suffering' (S 12, 15, 6 II p. 17). He who is convinced of non-selfness has already taken a big step towards the annihilation of suffering, for what could shake a man who knows that no event concerns 'him'?

Right View furthermore consists in discarding the Four Perverse Views (*vipallāsa*), which are: looking for something permanent in the impermanent, for happiness in suffering, for a Self in the non-self and for beauty in what is ugly (A 4, 49, 1 II p. 52).

(2) Right Resolve (*sammā-saṅkappa*) has a triple division: resolve to renunciation, to benevolence and not to harm living beings (D 22, 21 II p. 312).

The 'morality' group is covered by the three following rules (3, 4 and 5). They aim mainly at the acquisition of kammic merit (*puñña*) which lays the foundation for better rebirth. But as they are directed inwards and outwards they also benefit other beings.

(3) Right Speech (*sammā-vāca*) is speech that does not consist of lies, gossip, abuse and idle talk (D 22, 21 II p. 312). Words should not be squandered on every subject:

> Those things seen . . . , by which the speaker's unwholesome mental phenomena (*dhamma*) increase and (his) wholesome mental phenomena decrease, those things should not be spoken of, so I say. Those things seen . . . , however, by which the speaker's unwholesome mental phenomena dwindle and (his) wholesome mental phenomena increase, those things should be spoken of, so I say.
>
> (A 4, 183, 3 II p. 173)

(4) Right Conduct (*sammā-kammanta*) means desisting from taking of life, from taking things not given and from debaucheries (D 22, 21 II p. 312). How seriously these prohibitions are taken is shown by the monastic code which for their disregard imposes the severest disciplinary punishment inflicted for only four offences, namely expulsion from the order.

In the case of murder the unrobing places the monk under

secular jurisdiction where as any other layman he is brought to trial.

The intentional killing of an animal by a monk, however, is punished leniently and without discrimination as to whether the victim was a cow or a mosquito. The subtler punishment is left to the *kamma* which will differentiate between the action-intentions in both cases.

Theft committed by a *bhikkhu* is considered a reason for his expulsion where the same deed done by a layman would lead to conviction. Smaller offences against property are dealt with by disciplinary measures.

The harshest punishment again threatens a monk for actual or attempted unchastity. The lay follower on the other hand is only asked not to cool his passion—if he has to yield to it—with a girl under the protection of her parents and relatives, with married women or with prostitutes (M 41 I p. 286).

(5) Right Livelihood (*sammā-ājīva*) implies the pursuit of a harmless bread-winning which does not cause suffering to others:

> Monks, these five trades ought not to be followed by a lay follower. Which five?—: Trade in weapons, trade in living beings, trade in meat, trade in liquor, and trade in poison.
> (A 5, 177 III p. 208)

Professions incompatible with Right Livelihood are: sheep or pig butcher, fowler, trapper, hunter, fisherman, robber, executioner and jailer (M 51 I p. 343).

Although the professions of butcher and meat merchant are not allowed, the conclusion that this entails vegetarianism for all followers of the Dhamma is incorrect. Naturally, a serious seeker will reduce or stop eating meat out of compassion for the animals, but in doing so he cannot refer to an injunction of the Buddha. Not even the monk who is given meat in his alms bowl is forbidden to eat it unless he knows that the animal was slaughtered especially for him.

Gotama's statements about the proper conduct in professional life are remarkable. He considers that excessive poverty causes theft, violence and murder (D 26, 14 III p. 68). He explains to a man nicknamed 'Longknee' that four things are conducive to worldly well-being: professional proficiency, protection of property against loss, good company and a standard of living in accordance with the size of one's income (A 8, 54 IV p. 281 f.). When budgeting he advises that one quarter be used for sustenance, half for business transactions and the last quarter for savings (D 31, 26 III p. 188).

The last three categories of the Eightfold Way are subsumed under the heading of 'meditation'. 'Meditation' should be understood here in a general sense as a method of mental discipline.

(6) Right Effort (*sammā-vāyāma*) is defined as the endeavour to ward off unwholesome mental phenomena and to produce wholesome ones (D 22, 21 II p. 312). It's most important exercise is the 'guarding of the sense-gates' in order to train for pure, i.e. objective, observation:

> When . . . a monk sees with his eye a form, he clings neither to the total appearance nor to details. Since desire or aversion, bad and unwholesome mental phenomena overpower him who lives without control of the eye consciousness, he strives for its control. He guards the eye consciousness (and finally) brings about (its) control . . .
> When he has heard a sound with his ear . . . , smelled a scent with his nose . . . , savoured a taste with his tongue . . . , felt a tactile object with his body . . . , conceived a mental object with his thought, he clings neither to the total appearance nor to details . . . (D 2, 64 I p. 70)

The meaning of this instruction is not immediately evident.

With any sense-perception two factors are to be kept apart: the stimulus and the emotional reaction to it. Any attempt at shutting out the stimuli by switching off the senses is hopeless, since all beings require functioning sense-organs for the preservation of life. However, the reactions to these stimuli are controllable. Instead of letting them grow into sympathy and repulsion, desire and hatred the seeker has to make them objects of mental analysis and thereby causes them to fade away.

Simultaneously he endeavours to apply to the object of perception only descriptive and non-evaluating terms; the affective judgement 'desirable' for example is replaced by the neutral statement 'tall, dark-haired, full-bosomed'. After some practice he is able to perceive things without allowing their 'beauty' or 'ugliness' to create in him feelings of greed or aversion. He who masters this discipline, stating things with equanimity, objectively and without self-reference, and has made it a habit, has already fulfilled one of the two aspects of wisdom; for wisdom comprises both knowledge and supremacy over the stimuli of the world. Loving-kindness which the Buddhist is asked to show towards all beings must likewise not be an emotion grown from sense-perceptions, but a virtue which he develops out of free resolve.

(7) Right Awareness (*sammā-sati*) or Attentiveness means mindfulness of the body, sensations, mind and mental objects. It is a cure for states of agitation. A person who in a fit of rage becomes conscious of his outburst is already on his way to inner balance.

Attentiveness plays a special role in the 'Awakening of Awareness' (*satipaṭṭhāna*), a meditation exercise which is described in two suttas of the Pāli canon (D 22 and M 10) and enjoys extraordinary esteem in Theravādic countries. Its aim is to lift usually un- or semiconscious actions like breathing, walking, standing, sitting, lying, etc. into the light of full awareness. After having become aware of the body in this manner, one proceeds analogously with sensations, thoughts and mental phenomena. The purpose is to achieve concentration and to bring the fickle mind under control.

In these two suttas the *sati* technique does not appear in its pure form. It is mixed with other techniques belonging to the last member of the Eightfold Way, namely:

(8) Right Meditation (*sammā-samādhi*). It promotes under-

Gotama in meditation. (After a Tibetan bronze, probably 17th century.)

standing to distinguish between the *techniques* of meditation for which the Pāli canon employs special terms, and *exercises* of meditation which are composed of the techniques.

The techniques of (a) 'guarding of the sense-gates' (= sixth category of the Eightfold Way) and (b) 'Awakening of Awareness' (= seventh category) have already been mentioned. The other four are (c) focused observation, (d) trance, (e) contemplation and (f) abiding.

(c) Focused observation (*bhāvanā*) is the method to pinpoint the mind upon one selected object of the outer world. Suitable objects, for example, are a lump of earth, a coloured disc or a corpse in the various stages of disintegration.

(d) Trance (*samādhi* in a narrow sense or *jhāna*) is subdivided into eight stages. Two of these, the sixth and seventh, Gotama adopted from his former teachers Āḷāra Kālāma and Uddaka Rāmaputta—if he did not teach only the first four stages. It is possible that the other four have been incorporated into Buddhism by the compilers of the Pāli texts who borrowed them from other systems, especially from Yoga of which the Buddha's two teachers were also adherents.

The stages of trance are:

(i) Attentive pondering, free from sensual desires, and reflection with the feeling of well-being.
(ii) Cessation of pondering; inner stillness and mental concentration on *one* object with the feeling of well-being.
(iii) Equanimity, devotion, and clarity-of-knowledge.
(iv) Drying up of all feelings of bliss and suffering and of the recollection of them; equanimity and devotion of greatest purity.
(v) Termination of the perception of forms and shapes; experience of the infinity of space.
(vi) Experience of the 'infinity of consciousness' (i.e. experience that consciousness is all-pervasive).
(vii) Realisation of the essential no-thing-ness of all empirical things.
(viii) State of 'neither-perception-nor-non-perception' (= deep trance).

Occasionally a ninth stage is mentioned which can last up to seven days. By withdrawing thought and senses from the world or even switching them off temporarily the meditator obtains in his inner calm a foretaste of liberation.

(e) Contemplations (*anupassanā*) always have for their subject the Buddhist conception of things, be it the world (e.g. the saṃsāric marks of impermanence, sorrowfulness and non-selfness), man (e.g. the components and repulsiveness of the body), or the Dhamma (e.g. Conditioned Origination, the maturing of *kamma*, the way to deliverance, etc.). They pre-suppose familiarity with the Buddhist texts, for they should transform acquired knowledge into experienced reality.

(f) The Four Divine Abidings (*brahma-vihāra*) mean that the meditator produces successively in himself loving-kindness, compassion, joy and equanimity and radiates these feelings onto all beings in the six directions (including above and below). The idea is that these irradiations have a tangible effect on beings; it is reported that even an elephant attacking the

Buddha was appeased when the master radiated loving-kindness (*mettā*) towards it. The Abidings are often practised jointly by a group.

With reference to the meditational techniques 'b' to 'e' the Buddhist scriptures make a remarkable distinction. For all these techniques can be used as psychological tools and as means of gaining knowledge. When practised for the purpose of excluding distracting stimuli by narrowing the field of observation, they pacify (*samatha*) thought. However, when used to penetrate the chosen object analytically by most intensive observation, their result is Insight (*vipassanā*) or intuitive comprehension. It is easy to understand why the *vipassanā* method is considered the higher one.

Not all of the numerous meditations are suitable for everybody, and there are, moreover, people who are entirely without talent for them. In the case of a man gifted for meditation it should be observed which of the three main samsāric forces is predominant in him. To a greedy person the meditation master may perhaps recommend Contemplation on Non-selfness, to a person full of hatred the Abiding in Loving-kindness, to a deluded man the Awakening of the Awareness of Breathing. The treatment is always allopathical.

Buddhist authors usually stress the importance of the Eightfold Way for liberation from suffering. Undoubtedly this is appropriate for the majority of people who are footweary walkers towards deliverance. Yet the Buddhist scriptures also mention others who, without having followed the Eightfold Way consciously, have reached the goal after a single instruction on the Dhamma. They were particularly well qualified by *kamma* and of such a high mental calibre that by insight alone they were able to annihilate the forces that cause rebirth. Decisive for liberation is the rooting out of ignorance, craving, hatred and delusion, not the Eightfold Way in itself, which is merely a means thereto.

As can be seen the Eightfold Way exclusively enumerates precepts, that is rules of conduct which bring men closer to liberation. Early in the history of Buddhism, however, demand arose for a list of actions (*kamma*) to be avoided, as they lead to lower forms of rebirth. This catalogue consists of Ten Prohibitions, the first five of which are binding on all Buddhists, lay followers as well as monks. Prohibitions 6 to 10 are more of a disciplinary than an ethical nature and apply only to wearers of the yellow robe.

(1) Avoidance of destroying life,
(2) abstention from taking what has not been given,
(3) abstention from unchastity,
(4) abstention from lies,
(5) abstention from taking intoxicating drinks,
(6) abstention from eating after midday,
(7) keeping away from dancing, singing, music and the theatre,
(8) avoidance of garlands, perfumes, cosmetics and jewellery,
(9) disuse of lofty and luxurious couches,
(10) non-acceptance of gold and silver.

Though assigning great importance to morality (*sīla*), Gotama sets more value on loving-kindness (*mettā*) towards all beings. It is understood as a purification exercise promoting liberation rather than as self-abandonment:

> Whatever treasures of meritorious deeds there may be fundamental (for the kammic future), altogether they are worth not even one sixteenth of loving-kindness (which is) emancipation of thought. Loving-kindness transcends them; it shines and glows and radiates . . .
>
> . . .
>
> If with a well-disposed mind somebody shows loving-kindness towards one single being, he obtains happiness. He who with compassionate mind (shows loving-kindness) towards *all* beings, this noble person creates (for himself) abundant merit. (Itiv 27 pp. 19 + 21)

The most famous Buddhist document about loving-kindness is the *Mettāsutta* which in South East Asia is recited every day by millions. Although addressed to the monks, it is of no less importance for the lay followers.

Mettāsutta (The Sutta of Loving-Kindness)

1. This is how One who strives for happiness
   and wants to reach that quiet place,[15] should act:
   He should be able, upright, free from pride
   and thoughtful; likewise be his speech.
2. (He is) contented, easy to support,[16]
   unbusy, modest, and intelligent;
   he reins his senses, and with families
   is not demanding, soon to satisfy.
3. He (by no means) pursues a trifling goal
   that others, wise men, had to blame him for:
   All beings may reach happiness and peace,
   they all should grow (as) happy (as can be)!
4. Whatever beings live here (in this world),
   no matter whether they are strong or weak,
   procumbent or (with bodies) standing up,
   (of stature) small, or medium, firm or frail,
5. Living in hiding or in open view,
   dwelling nearby or (dwelling) farther off,
   already born or still in future's womb—:
   May all (these) beings come to happiness!
6. He never should abuse somebody nor
   despise (in any way) him anywhere;
   from anger and from enmity one must
   not wish for one another (harm or) ill.
7. Just like a mother at the risk of life
   (tries to) protect her son, her only child,
   just so should he towards *all* beings make
   his own mind free from (any) boundaries.
8. He should develop loving-kindness for
   the entire world and free his mind from bounds

[15] Nibbāna.

[16] This stanza admonishes the monks to modesty on their alms-collecting rounds.

in upward, downward and in level course,
unhindered, free from hatred and from spite.

9. He may be standing, walking, sitting (even) lying, —
in any posture that keeps indolence away
he ought to exercise this mindfulness.[17]:
This is Divine Abiding in this world.

10. By not adhering to perverted views,
by following the precepts, and with knowledge
he overcomes the craving after lust:
He will no more descend to any womb.

(Snip I, 8 = Khp 9)

Loving-kindness (*mettā*) and compassion (*karuṇā, anukampā*) give to ethics that warmth of life without which they remain stony and cold. Even when robbers and murderers are sawing off the limbs of a Buddhist monk—if this monk develops a feeling of enmity he is not fulfilling the Buddha's injunction. Even in this situation monks should behave thus:

> Our thinking will not be upset, and we will not utter one evil word. We will abide friendly and compassionate with a mind of loving-kindness, void of inner aversion. Having penetrated that person with a mind of loving-kindness, we will remain (in this state). Beginning with that (person), having penetrated the whole world with a mind of loving-kindness which is expanded, dedicated, limitless, peaceful (and) non-binding, we will remain (in this state).
>
> (M 21 I p. 129)

It is a peculiarity of Theravāda Buddhism that everyone has to obtain liberation through his own efforts and that the possibility of assistance from without is denied except for instruction about the Way. Neither prayer nor belief in heavenly beings can hasten deliverance from suffering, for the natural law of *kamma* is incorruptible. Nevertheless, faith (*saddhā*), or, more

[17] *Sati* here refers to the exercise (described in stanza 8) of radiating loving-kindness to the six regions: the meditation of Divine Abiding.

accurately, trusting confidence in the Buddha, also plays a role in the Theravāda. Without confidence in the master and the truth of his teaching no beginner would subject himself to the difficulties of the Eightfold Way. Without trusting confidence, therefore, no one could ever reach liberation.

12. THE GOAL: NIBBĀNA

A person who has walked the Eightfold Way to its end and so has reached enlightenment and liberation—a goal that can be realised by women no less than by men—becomes a saint (*arahant*). He differs only from a Buddha in that he owes his deliverance to instruction. The honorary title 'Buddha' is reserved for those who realise salvation through their own insight, that is without tuition. A Buddha who keeps his knowledge for himself is called in the Pāli texts a 'Private (*pacceka*) Buddha'; the one who expounds the Dhamma to others is a 'Perfect (*sammāsam*) Buddha'.

The Pāli sources contain abundant information about the state of a person who has reached Nibbāna, 'extinction'. However, affirmative attributes appear only in the edifying and poetic passages of the canon. Here Nibbāna is characterised as happiness, peace, security, bliss, deathlessness, purity, truth, health and the permanent. All these expressions make it clear that Nibbāna is not understood as nothingness but regarded as something positive.

The philosophical sections of the canon do not contradict this, but use negating statements since extinction is primarily freedom: the destruction of all factors binding to Saṃsāra and suffering. So the *Dīghanikāya* defines *Nibbāna* as eradication of the craving that causes rebirth (D 14, 3, 1 II p. 36), as emancipation from the three basic defilements greed, hatred and delusion (D 16, 4, 43 II p. 136), from which deeds arise which effect rebirth, and as the quieting down of the action-intentions (D 14, 3, 1 II p. 36), which are the originators of new forms of existence. Nibbāna cannot be achieved through deeds (*kamma*), through the utilisation of the law of *kamma*, and is not the destination of the kammic way, but is emancipation from kammic fetters. Whereas the forms of existence in the Six Realms of Rebirth are 'conditioned by action-intentions' (*saṅkhata*), Nibbāna is 'unobtainable by action-intentions' (*asaṅkhata*). For this very reason it is free from origination, decline and change (A 3, 47 I p. 152).

But Nibbāna does not mean the abandonment of negative qualities alone; the liberated one must also discard cherished ideals: the striving for Nibbāna and the teaching of the Buddha. For since Nibbāna as the termination of all craving and desire can only materialise when it has ceased to be the object of desire, intense longing for liberation is a hindrance to liberation. Nibbāna is only realisable in the absence of too eager an intent to reach it. And since, moreover, all mental values, as soon as they are obtained, become permanent possessions dear to the heart of the owner, the doctrine of the Buddha must also be relinquished in Nibbāna. When the river of suffering is crossed and the shore of deliverance reached, the doctrine as a raft to emancipation has become useless (M 22 I p. 135).

In spite of all their differences Nibbāna and the empirical person still have one thing in common: they both are and have no Self:

> Transient are all components of the personality (*saṅkhāra*),[18] sorrowful, not a Self and conditioned by action-intentions (*saṅkhata*). And Nibbāna too is something without a Self, this is certain. (Vin V p. 86 v. 1)

According to whether the extinguished and liberated person is still alive or has already died, a distinction is made between pre-mortal and post-mortal Nibbāna. In the former those factors are destroyed which bind to the cycle or rebirth; in the

[18] '*Saṅkhāra*' is a collective term for the Five Groups (*khandha*) constituting the personality when it is emphasised that these are *saṅkhata*: kammically created by the action-intentions (*saṅkhāra*) of previous existences. When used for the empirical person '*saṅkhāra*'—(lit. 'composition')—reminds one that the person is a combination of the Five Groups.

latter the liberated one is also dissolved as a perceiving being (Itiv 44 p. 38). Post-mortal Nibbāna is referred to as 'perfect extinction' (*parinibbāna*).

In pre-mortal Nibbāna the liberated one is characterised by unshakable evenmindedness. He is not beyond physical susceptibility but the term 'suffering' no more applies to him: As he has mentally realised non-selfness nothing can worry 'him' any longer. Knowing that he has escaped saṃsāric enchainment, he lives for *parinibbāna*.

Yet his state ought not to be confused with inactivity and apathy. Only the motives entangling him in Saṃsāra have ceased to exist. Positive impulses like kindness, compassion and wisdom have by no means died out in him. They make him not only a model for his environment, but also a person of practical helpfulness.

The concept of post-mortal Nibbāna shows how closely the Buddhist notion of liberation and the doctrine of non-self are related. Had Gotama asserted the existence of a Soul, this Soul as something eternal would continue to exist even in Parinibbāna, and Parinibbāna would be some kind of paradise in which the liberated souls find peace. But as Gotama teaches the soullessness of the empirical person, Parinibbāna is just the disintegration of the Five Groups, which in combination composed the person of the liberated one. The death of a liberated being is final, no new 'Groups' can arise, his chain of rebirths is broken off for good.

The criticism raised against the Buddha that he is a teacher of annihilation (*venayika*) as he propagated the destruction of the person, misses the point. For since he regards the personality merely as a phenomenon and not as something in essence, there can be no question of the destruction of a 'person' in Parinibbāna. Rightly the Buddha protests against this censure:

> Of what I am not, monks, of what I do not say, of that these venerable ascetics and brahmins wrongly accuse me. . . . Formerly and today, monks, I teach but one thing: suffering and the termination of suffering. (M 22 I p. 140)

This defence is convincing only for someone who has fully understood the equation: Nexus of Conditioned Origination = empirical person = suffering.

The Pāli texts describe the inner as well as the outer condition of the liberated one after death. As is to be expected they do so chiefly by way of negations.

As with the disintegration of the empirical person in Parinibbāna the apperceiving consciousness finds its end, the world, too, ceases to exist for the liberated one. For him, so the Buddha explains, Nibbāna is

> the sphere where there is neither earth nor water nor fire nor air; neither the sphere of the infinity of space nor the sphere of the infinity of consciousness nor the sphere of nothingness nor the sphere of non-perception or perception; neither this world nor a world yonder nor both, nor sun and moon. I declare, monks, that there is no coming and going, neither duration nor destruction nor origination. It is without basis, development and condition. This is the end of suffering. (Ud 8, 1 p. 80)

To the question of Udāyi as to how this state, this Nibbāna, in which all sensation has stopped, can be called happiness, the monk Sāriputta replies:

> Just this *is* the happiness . . . that there is no more sensation! (A 9, 34, 3 IV p. 415)

A description of the perfect liberated one is beyond all possibilities of language. One can neither say that the Perfect One exists in Parinibbāna nor that he does not exist (D 15, 32 II p. 68). The Five Groups composing the empirical person which one could have in mind when talking of the liberated one—of these Five Groups he has ridded himself and they can never arise again (M 72 I p. 487 f.). The best simile for the liberated one is that of a fire of which after its extinction (*nibbāna*) no one can say where it has gone:

Just like a flame blown out by a strong wind
'goes home' and so defies all definition,
just so a sage, from Name and Body freed,
'goes home' and can no longer be defined.
(Snip 1074)

Neither are the senses nor is the mind able to descry one who has entered Parinibbāna (S 35, 83 IV p. 52 f.). The perfect liberated being is beyond comprehensibility:

For the Extinguished One there is no measure
and nothing is there to define him by;
when all appearances come to an end
the ways of language, too, have reached a stop.
(Snip 1076)

The Main Schools of the Hīnayāna

During the Second Council which took place in Vesālī approximately one hundred years after the Buddha's death, that is about 383 B.C., the Buddhist order split into two schools: the Theravādins (Skt.: Sthaviravādins), 'Followers of the Teaching of the Elders', and the Mahāsāṅghikas (Skt.), the 'Great Community'. The Theravādins claim to possess the unadulterated tradition of the Buddha's word, and it is their canon which in complete form is handed down to us in Pāli. Of the canon of the Mahāsāṅghikas which was written in the so-called hybrid Sanskrit, i.e. Sanskrit interspersed with dialectisms, only one work, the *Mahāvastu*, is extant today.

The reasons for the schism of the order are adequately known. According to one source it was a disagreement about ten disciplinary rules which caused the breach; according to another it was the concept of the Buddhist saint (*arahant*). In opposition to the conservative monks one group of them took the view that even saints are exposed to temptations and not necessarily omniscient. In contrast to the ideal of the world-transcending saint they created that of the world-sympathising Bodhisattva. When no agreement could be reached the innovators united and so formed the school of the Mahāsāṅghikas.

In other points also the Mahāsāṅghikas differed from the Theravādins. They no longer looked upon the Buddha as an ordinary human being but as a superman; they asserted that suffering could not only be eliminated by virtuous conduct and enlightenment but also by wisdom alone; they considered the mind of the reborn being as not constricted by old *kamma* but as being free and pure; and created the concept of universal Emptiness. In scarcely modified form these features can later be found in the Mahāyāna.

Numerous sub-schools split off from the Theravāda and the Mahāsāṅghika in the course of the next two centuries. Tradition speaks of eighteen Hīnayānic schools, but the texts mention more than thirty by name. Only the most important ones will be listed here.

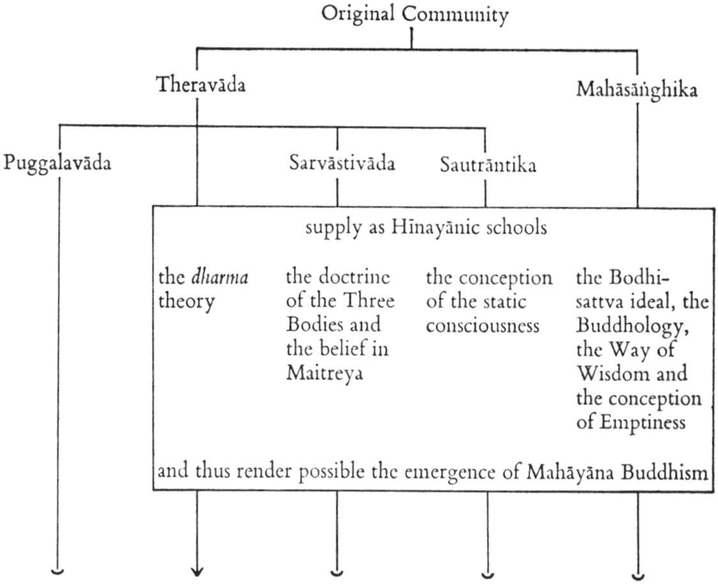

The Puggalavāda (Skt.: Pudgalavāda), the Sarvāstivāda (Skt.) and the Sautrāntika (Skt.) trace their origins back to the Theravāda. The Sarvāstivāda and the Sautrāntika possessed their own bodies of scriptures in Sanskrit, the main works of which are preserved in Chinese and Tibetan translations. The most important book of the Sarvāstivāda is the *Abhidharmakośa* of Vasubandhu (fifth century A.D.); its Sanskrit version was rediscovered in the 1950s.

Of the Hīnayāna schools the Puggalavāda is the one which deviates farthest from the orthodox tradition. It interpreted the sermons of the Buddha in such a way that there is, after all, something permanent in the cycle of rebirths, namely the 'person' (*puggala*). The person is neither identical with the Five Groups constituting the individual nor different from them. Like the Theravādins, the Puggalavādins theoretically denied the possibility of finding a Soul in the Five Groups, but in practice ascribed to the *puggala* all the attributes which would be peculiar to a Soul. The *puggala* was conceived as the beneficiary of the wholesome and sufferer of bad *kamma* and as continuing to exist even in Parinibbāna. In reply to their numerous opponents they referred to passages of the Pāli canon which in fact use the word 'person'—probably a case of careless language. The best-known Pāli Sutta of this kind is that of the burden (S 3, 1, 22 III p. 25 f.) in which the Five Groups are called the burden and the 'person' its carrier.

The Sarvāstivādins were not so much antagonists of the Theravādins as continuators of their teachings. Whereas the Theravādins only say that a Self, a Soul, can 'not be found' in the Five Groups, the Sarvāstivādins did not hesitate to deny the existence of a Soul outright (Ak 3, 18 p. 56). Like the Theravādins they explained the process of rebirth without a Soul by the Nexus of Conditioned Origination, but besides this they referred more often to the so-called *dharma* (P.: *dhamma*) theory—a doctrine which arose in the late Theravāda but is of importance only for Theravādic scholasticism. According to this theory all existing things are reduced to *dharmas*, 'factors of existence', in the sense of last principles or basic realities.

From the start one has to keep apart two groups of Dharmas. The small group consists of the Non-conditioned (*asaṃskṛta*) Dharmas which form the state of liberation. They are eternal, that is not conditioned by karmic causes, and are not subject to the formative power of *karman*. In the Theravāda only Nirvāṇa (P.: *nibbāna*) is considered a Non-conditioned Dharma. The Sarvāstivāda counts three Non-conditioned Dharmas, other schools up to nine. They do not participate in the dharma process, that is in the creation of this sorrowful world.

Set against these few Non-conditioned Dharmas are all the Conditioned (*saṃskṛta*) Dharmas. What are these Conditioned Dharmas, how does the dharma process function and which powers propel it?

The Buddhist schools have devoted great pains to the counting and classification of the Dharmas (lit. 'bearers'). Whereas the number of the Dharmas—listed are 75, 84 or 100—is of no

Head of meditating Buddha. (After a Thai sculpture of the 13th century.)

importance the classifications are valuable since they make clear the nature of the Dharmas. As Conditioned Dharmas (= factors of existence) are understood:

1. the sensual or perceptive faculties, the corresponding sense-spheres, namely the visible, audible, etc. and the contents of perception;
2. consciousness and thought-activity;
3. the innate abilities and talents of an individual as well as his moods, emotions, impulses and interests—in short, the psychic processes;
4. non-physical relations and processes like obtaining, non-obtaining, vitality, ageing, impermanence, etc.

As the dharma theory purports, all empirical beings and all that is reflected in them as the external world are but phenomena formed by Conditioned Dharmas. The Dharmas are the structural elements of empirical existence that cannot be further reduced. Caused and steered by *karman* they combine in certain ratios and so form the phenomena which we experience as ourselves and as the world. The whole of reality is exhausted in the phenomena constituted by the Conditioned Dharmas. There is no substratum, no 'true reality' or 'essence' behind or beyond them.

The special characteristic of the Conditioned Dharmas which alone qualifies them to enact the dharma process is the shortness of their activity. With regard to the nature of the Dharmas the Theravāda and the Sarvāstivāda schools hold divergent views.

The Theravādins see the Conditioned Dharmas as short-lived. Dharmas arise, combine with others into dharma-groups or phenomena and vanish in order to give way to new Dharmas and new phenomena. The Conditioned Dharmas as the Theravāda understands them are comparable to the individual sounds of a melody. No sound exists longer than for the fraction of a second during which it can be heard, but just this makes it possible for the sounds to supersede each other in quick succession and thus effect the appearance of a melody.—It was pre-eminently in this form that the dharma theory was taken over by the Mahāyāna.

The Sarvāstivādins view the nature of the Conditioned Dharmas differently. According to them the Dharmas are also effective for only a short time; however, they do not originate, but have existed from time immemorial: they merely change from latency to activity. The process suggests comparison with a film. Though the pictures on the film strip are permanent they are active only in the moment of projection. The sequence of activity flashes of different pictures makes up that which is experienced as life action.

The Sarvāstivādins themselves explain the functioning of the Dharmas by the example of a stone on a mountain peak. For a long time the stone lies there ineffective. One day it begins to fall, becomes effective, until it comes to rest in the valley and slides back once more into ineffectiveness.—The stone on the peak is comparable to a Dharma of the future, while falling it is like a Dharma of the present, when come to rest again it is a Dharma of the past. In the stone—as in the Dharmas—the three times are not dead: past, present and future co-exist in them. 'All (that ever was and will be) *is*' (*sarvam asti*)—that is the axiom of the Sarvāstivādins from which the school took its name.

It helps understanding to distinguish between the individual dharma process and the super-individual one.

The individual dharma process explains the throbbing of life in man, the constant change of his consciousness and the fluctuation of the contents of his thought. The Dharmas which by their kaleidoscopic combinations constitute thinking are of shortest duration—the scholastics measure them by thousandths of an eyeblink. As the Buddha understands by 'world' that which in human consciousness is reflected as such, the dharma process also suffices to explain the personal world, for how the world looks to us depends on the dharma-conglomeration which composes our mind. The individual dharma process is a psychological theory with a partly ontological function.

The super-individual dharma process supplies the theoretical foundation to rebirth without a Soul. Dharmas come into being due to karmic preconditions and on account of this very karman unite to compose an individual. When the Dharmas, which today constitute Peter, disintegrate on his death, the action-intentions which Peter had fostered while alive determine which new Dharmas will unite in 'his' new form of existence—which may perhaps be called Paul. Paul is in no way identical with Peter, but owes to Peter what he is, and without him would never have stepped into life. For the Dharmas karman is a causing as well as a formative power. With regard to the latter one is reminded of the school experiment with iron filings which in a magnetic field are mysteriously arranged in a pattern.

Like scarcely any other thought element of Buddhism the interpretation of the personality as a dynamic stream of Conditioned Dharmas is apt to root out the belief in a Soul, a permanent Self or Ego. Expressions like 'suffering', '*karman*', and 'liberation' which are used so frequently in Buddhism, do indeed relate to a subject, but this is only an empirical one: a dharma combination, nothing in essence. The Pāli scholastic Buddhaghosa (fifth century A.D.) illustrates this by some stanzas which he pretends to quote, but probably has composed himself:

There is suffering but no sufferer,
there is the deed, but no doer is there,
extinction is, but none who is extinct,
there is no walker, but the Way.

(Vism 16 II p. 513)

There is no doer of *kamma*
and none who reaps its result:
What moves are but the Dhammas—
thus (knows he who) comprehends aright.

(Vism 19 II p. 602)

To the Mahāyāna the Sarvāstivādins contributed an early form of the doctrine of the Three Bodies, the basic idea of which they had taken over from the Mahāsāṅghikas. They also introduced the belief in the future Buddha Maitreya (P.: Metteya), which in the Theravāda is of subordinate, in the Sarvāstivāda of greater, significance.

The Sautrāntikas bear that name as they rejected the Abhidharma part of the Sanskrit canon and relied exclusively on its Sūtra part (*sūtrānta*). Like the Theravādins they held that the Conditioned Dharmas exist only as long as they are effective, but behind the chain of Dharmas they assumed a substratum (*āśraya*), namely a consciousness acting as a continuum (*santāna*, *santati*). This timeless consciousness forms, so to speak, a rail for the Five Groups which constitute the person. According to the Sautrāntikas these Five Groups continue to exist after death in subtle form and move over along the rail of consciousness to the next rebirth. By developing the idea of a static consciousness the Sautrāntikas supplied the central concept for the monistic idealism of the Yogācāra system.

III

MAHĀYĀNA—THE MONISTIC BUDDHISM OF LIBERATION BY 'OTHER-POWER'[19]

Hīnayāna and Mahāyāna—Contrasts and Similarities

About four hundred years after the Buddha's passing away a new form of Buddhism appeared in India which calls itself Mahāyāna, 'Great Vehicle' (across the ocean of suffering). It points out new ways to emancipation and thus makes this supreme goal accessible to a wider range of human types than did the older Buddhism for which the derogatory name Hīnayāna or 'Small Vehicle' now comes in use. As the Mahāyānins allege the Hīnayāna is merely the introductory part of the teaching of the Buddha: unconcentrated as his former audience had been they were only able to absorb a fragment of his teaching (SP 3 p. 47). Conversely, the Hīnayānins call the Mahāyāna a distortion of what Gautama had taught.

Following up the differences between Hīnayāna and Mahāyāna in detail, it appears that almost all elements which seem 'typically Mahāyānic' are traceable already in Hīnayāna. The most prominent differences between the two branches of Buddhism are the following:

(1) In relation to the reality of the world the Hīnayāna holds a psychological realism, the Mahāyāna an idealism. Consequently the Hīnayāna regards suffering as real, the Mahāyāna as an illusion (which, however, only the sage recognises as such).

[19] From this chapter onwards all Indian terms and names are given in Sanskrit.

(2) In contrast to the Hīnayāna which denies a 'true being' behind phenomena and avoids making metaphysical statements, the Mahāyāna teaches an Eternal Absolute under a great variety of names. This Absolute is not transcendent but something imminent in Saṃsāra. Even in the dharmas, which by the Hīnayāna are considered mere phenomenal entities, the Mahāyāna is able to see the Absolute: in their emptiness.

Likewise the Mahāyāna looks at the beings in all forms of rebirth as identical in their cores with the Absolute (and consequently with each other). The Mahāyāna is monistic, and the constant accentuation of non-duality its special note.

(3) The historical Buddha Gautama is interpreted in the Mahāyāna as a projection of the Absolute. He is in essence identical with the Last Principle, but illusion in his frail mortal frame. In the Hīnayāna he is regarded as a natural man and teacher, at the most a superman.

(4) As against the Hīnayāna view that liberation can only be achieved by one's own efforts, the Mahāyāna considers assistance from outside as possible; it concedes deliverance through 'other-power'.

(5) The Mahāyāna teaches the transference of karmic merit to other persons and thus breaks the strict causality of the Hīnayānic law of *karman* (P.: *kamma*) according to which everybody wanting better rebirth can reach it solely by his own efforts. On this point, however, Mahāyāna and Hīnayāna differ only in the texts. The religious practice in South East Asia acknowledges the transference of karmic merit (P.: *pattidāna*) in Theravāda as well.

(6) The Hīnayānins, with the exception of the Mahāsāṅghikas, see their immediate goal in reaching personal extinction: nirvāṇa (P.: *nibbāna*). Most of the Mahāyānins on the other hand have set themselves the intermediate goal of Bodhisattvahood in order to lead *all* beings to liberation. To them their own extinction and liberation are of secondary importance.

(7) Nirvāṇa—in the Hīnayāna understood as victory over *Saṃsāra* and the final exit from the world—is in the Mahāyāna taken as the becoming conscious of one's own absoluteness

(= liberation) and is a state of mental aloofness from, but within, the world which does not exclude active endeavour for the liberation of other beings. The Hīnayānin has to create Nirvāṇa, the Mahāyānin is in essence liberated from the very beginning. In the Absolute which he presages in himself he already possesses Buddhahood and has merely to become aware of this fact by experience.

(8) The Hīnayāna and the Mahāyāna moreover differ in their basic attitudes towards life. The Hīnayāna intends to *surmount* the world: by analysing its elements and utilising the resulting knowledge for individual conduct. The Mahāyāna on the other hand wants to *help* the world: it educates its followers to selfless effort for others and allows them to have recourse to transcendent powers. The Hīnayānic thinking in terms of natural categories is in the Mahāyāna relinquished in favour of the experience of the supernatural. Whereas Hīnayāna has a rational, the Mahāyāna has a meta-rational, attitude; inference stands against paradox, reason against wisdom.

These material differences between the two branches of Buddhism entail a contrast in their fluidic atmospheres which is more easily sensed than described. The Hīnayāna attracts by its pragmatic approach, by its soberness and immanence-thinking, the Mahāyāna by the emotional warmth of its ethics and the colourfulness of its spiritual world. The Hīnayānin is like a vigorous man who, though tired from a long journey, is striding out under bright sunshine towards a distant goal which he wants to reach soon. The Mahāyānin resembles a mature man who without haste moves about in his spacious house to which portraits in dark colours on the walls and old books impart an occult atmosphere. He who wishes to join the former man will be called to take long strides and not to waste time. He who wants to join the Mahāyānin, however, will be invited by him for a discussion about the task of being human—and for a cup of tea.

So far the differences between Hīnayāna and Mahāyāna have been dealt with. But what do the two branches of Buddhism have in common, what binds them together as 'Buddhism'?

The characteristic features of all Buddhist schools are (1) the evaluation of individual existence as sorrowful and consequently requiring deliverance, (2) the belief in rebirth, (3) the assumption of a moral natural law which rules the process of *karman* and rebirth and was neither created by a deity nor is supervised by him, and (4) the view that the phenomenal world is without substance and in a constant flux. Analogous to this (5) the empirical person is considered as without Self and as a complex of soulless factors, with which (6) the goal of extinction of the sorrowful personality is logically connected. Further characteristics are (7) the conviction that liberation is only achievable through the extirpation of greed, hatred and delusion and by gaining enlightenment (= wisdom) and lastly (8) faithful confidence in the Buddhas, be they regarded as human teachers, supermen or transcendent beings. Any doctrine which possesses *all* these features must be called Buddhistic.

The Sanskrit Literature of the Mahayana

The holy books of the Mahāyāna are called Sūtras, 'guide-*lines*'. Unlike the Hīnayānic Pāli Suttas, 'discourses' which rarely exceed twenty pages in print, many of the Mahāyāna-sūtras fill hundreds of pages. Their authors are anonymous.

If the Hīnayānic Suttas are valued only on account of their contents, the Mahāyānasūtras also possess beside that a 'magical' value. They are foci of transcendental power, for every truth irrespective of the weight of its content is effective.[20] How powerful then must be a book containing the full truth of the Buddha's doctrine! As a result of this view some Mahāyānic books contain hints that the work protects him who mentally masters it against assaults, heals his illnesses or fulfils his wishes —partly just those wishes the worthlessness of which is revealed in the text. One may discard the magical employment of Sūtras as superstition, but the idea behind it is a very positive one, namely that truth as a spiritual principle is always victorious.

By inner criteria two main groups can be distinguished in the Sūtra literature. To the one belong the devotional texts whose spiritual centre is in the Buddhology and the Bodhisattva teaching. They demand of the reader devoutness and faithful confidence in the Buddhas and have their origin in the Northern part of India. To the second belong the philosophical Sūtras. They deal mainly with the Absolute which is the essence of all Buddhas and beings. The areas of their origin are the Eastern parts of South and Middle India.

With reference to the age of the Sūtras scholars assume the period between the first century B.C. and the sixth century A.D. as that of their origination. Since all important texts were translated into Chinese and/or Tibetan at dates that were carefully

[20] The belief in the efficacy of truth for the obtainment of wishes is of pre-Buddhist origin, but has taken root in all schools of Buddhism. In the 'employment of truth' (*satyakriyā*, P.: *saccakiriyā*) the truth can also be a dogma, e.g. 'The Buddha is a precious jewel,—*through this truth* be happiness!'

recorded it is possible with most of them to tell when they must have existed at the latest.

The following list enumerates the more important Mahāyāna-sūtras which are extant in pure or hybrid Sanskrit and available in printed editions.

Daśabhūmika (= *Daśabhūmīśvara*)[21]
Gaṇḍavyūha[21]
Guṇakāraṇḍavyūha
Kāraṇḍavyūha
Karuṇāpuṇḍarīka
Kāśyapaparivarta[22]
Laṅkāvatāra
Prajñāpāramitā
Rāṣṭrapāla (*paripṛcchā*)[22]
Saddharmapuṇḍarīka
Śālistamba
Samādhirāja (= *Candrapradīpa*)
Sukhāvatīvyūha (in two recensions)
Suvarṇaprabhāsa (*uttama*)

The *Prajñāpāramitāsūtra* consists of about forty books or individual Sūtras of which the following are handed down in Sanskrit:

Adhyardhaśatikā (fragment)
Aṣṭādaśasāhasrikā
Aṣṭasāhasrikā
Hṛdaya (in two recensions)
Kauśikā
Mañjuśrīparivarta (= *Saptaśatikā*)
Pañcaviṃśatisāhasrikā
Ratnaguṇasaṃcayagāthā (= a versified condensation of the *Aṣṭasāhasrikā*)

[21] These Sūtras are portions of the (*Buddha-*) *Avataṃsakasūtra* composed of numerous individual works which is lost in Sanskrit and preserved only in Chinese and Tibetan.

[22] These two works are the only books preserved in Sanskrit of the Sūtra collection *Ratnakūṭa* which is handed down complete in Chinese and Tibetan.

The 'Vulture Peak' at Rājagaha. For strategic reasons Rājagaha, the capital of the old kingdom of Magadha, was built amidst mountains and consequently in the Indian summer was stifling hot and in the monsoon period humid and stuffy. Gotama, therefore, liked to spend his time on the Vulture Peak. Here he preached dozens of sermons. The platform on top of the rock is of later origin.

From the Vulture Peak the eye wanders back to the now uninhabited valley of Rājagaha. The modern town of Rājgir lies outside the valley. The ascent to the Vulture Peak begins at the remains of the monastery which Jīvaka, the physician in ordinary to king Bimbisāra of Magadha and, at behest of the king, also physician to the monastic order, presented to the Buddha as a gift. Further up on the path, perhaps on the road section in the picture, one passes the place where Devadatta tried in vain to kill the master by hurling down a boulder.
After the death of the Buddha (483 B.C.) the First Council took place in a cave in one of the mountains around Rājagaha.

Śatasāhasrikā
Suvikrāntavikrāmīparipṛcchā (= *Sārdhadvisāhasrikā*)
Svalpākṣara
Vajrachedikā (= *Triśatikā*).

There are indications that the *Aṣṭasāhasrikā*, which was composed in the first century B.C., is the oldest *Prajñāpāramitā* work from which all other *Prajñāpāramitās* originated. Many Mahāyāna monks revered the books of the *Prajñāpāramitā* even higher than they did the Buddha, for according to the teaching of these scriptures the Perfection (*pāramitā*) of Wisdom (*prajñā*) is the basis and the content of Buddhahood.

The philosophical Sūtras gave rise to the formation of philosophical schools and hence are regarded by them as ultimate authorities. The Madhyamaka school consolidated by Nāgārjuna is based on the *Prajñāpāramitā*—and the *Saddharma-puṇḍarīka-Sūtras*; the Yogācāra school founded by Maitreya (nātha) and Asaṅga on the Sūtras *Laṅkāvatāra*, *Avataṃsaka* and *Sandhinirmocana*. From both communities emerged thinkers whose treatises, the so-called Śāstras or 'textbooks', to a large extent remain to us. All Buddhist Śāstras were written between the second and the tenth century A.D.

The Basic Teachings of the Mahāyāna

I. THE BUDDHOLOGY

When in the year 483 B.C. the funeral pyre collapsed in whose flames the body of the Buddha had been cremated, the remembrance of the deceased began to detach from the historical facts; decades later it had in the minds of many Buddhists become transfigured into legend. Could a normal mortal possibly have discovered the universal laws formulated in the Teaching? Could a *human* bring deliverance to so many? Had Gotama not rather been a superman?—When at the Second Council (around 383 B.C.) the original community split into Theravādins and Mahāsāṅghikas the latter sanctioned this view. In the *Mahāvastu*, a voluminous Buddha 'biography' in which Gotama appears as a miracle-working hero, they gave their notion of the master's nature literary expression.

A second, later work, titled *Lalitavistara* and springing from the Sarvāstivāda school, carries the idealisation further and interprets the life of Gotama as a 'play' (*lalita*) of the essentially supramundane Buddha. The *Lalitavistara* stands at the point of transition from Hīnayāna to Mahāyāna.

In the *Saddharmapuṇḍarīkasūtra*, the 'Lotus of the Good Law', which was composed in the first century A.D. and incorporates older material, we finally encounter the Buddha in that concept which is characteristic of the Mahāyāna: as universal saviour and bestower of deliverance.

> Like a cloud, . . . which has risen above the world and, covering all, envelops the earth, (5)
> like this great cloud, filled with water and adorned with lightning, sounds its thunder and delights all beings (6)
> like it, (then) releases a mighty mass of water (and), raining all around, refreshes this earth (8)
> —just so the Buddha rises in the world like a cloud and after he, the Lord of the World, has arisen, he reveals to (all) beings the Right Conduct. (16)

> And thus declares the great seer who is worshipped in the (whole) world including the gods: 'I am the Perfect One, the best of men, the victor, arisen in the world like a cloud. (17)
> I wish refresh all beings whose members wither (and) who cling to the triple existence (in the three spheres of the world). Those who wither away in suffering I will lead to happiness; I will (fulfil) their wishes and give them peace (*nirvṛti*). (18)
> Listen to me, you crowds of gods and men, draw closer to see me! I am the Perfect One, the exalted, the highest; I was born here into the world for the liberation (of all beings).' (19)
> (SP 5 p. 61 f.)

As transcendent being the Buddha is master over space and time. He speaks of himself:

> Inconceivable thousands of millions of world-ages whose duration can never be fathomed is it since I first obtained enlightenment; (since then) I continually expound the teaching. (1)
> I seize (with the teaching) numerous Bodhisattvas and transpose them into *buddha*-knowledge. During many millions of world-ages I make many million myriads of beings mature (to enlightenment). (2)
> I delude (beings into seeing) the sphere of *Nirvāṇa*. As a means to (moral) discipline I tell beings (about it). I am, however, not extinct; I am here (in the world) and reveal the teaching. (3)
> When they (i.e. men) regard me as perfectly extinct (*parinirvṛta*), they offer manifold worship to the relics. They do not see me (and therefore) develop desire (for me). By that their minds become candid. (5)
> When beings are candid, gentle, forbearing and free from greed, then I hold a congregation of disciples and reveal myself (to them) on the Vulture Peak. (6)
> And then I speak thus to them: 'Monks, I am not extinct here (in this world). (My apparent extinction) was a clever

trick of mine (to encourage beings). Again and again I am born in the world of living beings.' (7) (SP 15 p. 211 f.)

According to this the earthly life of the Buddha Gautama and his nirvāṇa are illusions which the timeless and transcendent Buddha projected onto the world in order to lead mankind to knowledge and virtuous conduct.

In the exposition of his teaching the Buddha is absolutely impartial:

> With one (and the same) voice I declare the teaching (to all people) and always emphasise enlightenment as the final goal. For this is the same (for all beings), there is no partiality (in me); I hold neither sympathy nor antipathy (21).
> I refresh this whole world like a cloud which rains water uniformly (on everyone). The same enlightenment is for noblemen and lowborn, for the wicked as well as for the virtuous. (24) (SP 5 p. 62 f.)

Yet the Buddha is not visible to everybody. Whether someone is able to see him or not depends on his deeds (*karman*). About those who have burdened themselves with unwholesome karman, he says:

> Through many millions of world-ages they hear, when they are born, neither my name nor (that) of (other) Perfect Ones, neither that of the teaching nor that of my (monks') community. Thus is the fruit of bad action. (15)
> But when gentle and forbearing beings originate here in this world of man, then because of their good actions they see me revealing the teaching as soon as they are born. (16)
> (SP 15 p. 213)

Good actions (*karman*) or, more precisely, good action-intentions (*saṃskāra*) open man's eyes to see the Buddha and his ears to hear his teaching.

All passages quoted so far speak of only one Buddha. Is

Gautama then the only Buddha who appeared in the world? All Buddhist sources, Hīnayānic and Mahāyānic alike, negate this by naming other Buddhas besides Gautama. In Mahāyāna conviction there are as many Buddhas as grains of sand on the banks of the Ganges. In every world-system, every region of the world and in each age Perfect Ones do appear in order to show beings the Buddha-vehicle (*buddhayāna* = Mahāyāna) which leads to omniscience (SP 2 p. 31 f.).

2. THE DOCTRINE OF THE THREE BODIES

The Theravādins regarded the Buddhas as humans, the Mahāsāṅghikas saw them as super-humans, the Sarvāstivādins as heavenly beings. To harmonise these differences the Sarvāstivādins introduced the system of the Three Bodies (*tri-kāya*), which was later adopted by the Mahāyāna and fitted to its transcendent Buddha conception. According to this teaching above the Earthly Buddhas of gross-material physiques there are others of super-human nature with subtle physiques. Above these again ranks the *dharma*-principle, the immaterial Absolute which is immanent in everything. This *dharma* body is common to all the Buddhas.

The doctrine of the Three Bodies constitutes the spiritual skeleton of Mahāyānic Buddhology. In the old Sūtras it occurs in an archaic form. It was the philosophers of the Yogācāra who gave it its final shape.

I. *Dharmakāya*

The meaning of the term *dharma* varies according to the context. The word designates:

(a) The cosmic order, the natural law which rules our world, the mental-mechanical functional principle of existence to which everything must obey in order to be able to exist. In this sense the *dharma* is that which conditions all phenomena.

(b) The teaching of the Buddha in which this natural law is revealed and put into words. Since congruency between object and description is the criterion of truth, and Buddhism assumes full agreement between natural law and its verbal expression in the Buddha's teaching, *dharma* as 'teaching' connotes both 'truth' and 'reality'.

(c) Dharmas, furthermore, are called the norms of conduct which Gautama deduces from the natural law and whose observance is conducive to better rebirth. In short, *dharma* here is a name for karmically wholesome deeds.

(d) *Dharma* moreover are the partial manifestations of the natural law, namely 'facts' or 'things', be they meant directly or

(e) as reflections in the mind of an observer. In the latter connotation *dharma* must be translated by 'contents of thought', 'mental objects' or 'ideas'.

(f) Finally *dharma* is the technical term for the 'factors of existence' which from the time of the later Hīnayāna are regarded as the constructional elements of the empirical person and his subjective world. In this sense the word usually occurs in the plural.

As a part of the compound *dharmakāya*, (dharma-body), *dharma* is to be understood mainly in the meanings (a) and (b), but exceeds them in content. The Dharmakāya is the self-centred immanent as well as transcendent truth or reality of all beings and appearances: the indestructible, timeless Absolute, the one essence in and behind all that was, is, and will be. It is the bearer and the object of enlightenment or Buddhahood.

The Mahāyānic texts differentiate whether the Dharmakāya in the respective passage designates (i) the essence of the worldly beings or (ii) that of the Buddhas.

(i) In the first meaning the Dharmakāya is also called reality (*dharmatā*), core of reality (*dharmadhātu*), thusness (*tathatā*), thusness of existence (*bhūtatathatā*), essential body (*svabhāvakāya*), emptiness (*śūnyatā*) and base-consciousness (*ālayavijñāna*). The clearer the Dharmakāya is recognisable in a being the higher is this being's rank in the spiritual hierarchy.

(ii) When the Dharmakāya is looked upon as the inward nature of the Buddhas, it is styled Buddhaness (*buddhatā*), Buddha nature (*buddhasvabhāva*) and Matrix of the Perfect Ones (*tathāgatagarbha*).

The Dharmakāya is that one of the Three Bodies which all Buddhas have in common.[23] Whereas there existed and exist innumerable Earthly Buddhas and there are countless Transcendent Buddhas, there is only one Dharmakāya. Beings on a lower level of knowledge behold a multitude of Buddhas and see a contrast between the Buddhas and the phenomenal world. However, those who have attained enlightenment and transcendent wisdom experience in the Dharmakāya the essential identity and unity, not only of the Buddhas with each other, but also of the Buddhas with the beings of the world. It is this view which stamps the Mahāyāna as monistic.

The attempt to say more about the Dharmakāya is doomed to failure from the start. The Dharmakāya is without any distinguishing marks which render its description possible. It cannot even be explained by way of negations. This procedure would have to contrast it to something and thus take it as one pole of a bi-polarity. The Dharmakāya is, however, the absolute reality, besides which there is no other reality. However much the teachings of the Mahāyāna schools diverge from each other, they all identify the Absolute with the Dharmakāya.

There is, however, no unanimity about the nature of the Dharmakāya. Differing from the majority of the Sūtras which conceive it as something impersonal, as a neuter, some texts understand it as personal and attribute virtues to it, particularly that of compassion. Thus the *Laṅkāvatārasūtra* designates the Dharmakāya as Buddha of the Law (*dharma(tā)buddha*), Buddha with the Knowledge of a Perfect One (*tathāgatajñānabuddha*) or as the Perfect One who is the Root (*mūlatathāgata*). Certain Tantrayānic schools worship the Dharmakāya as the Primordial Buddha (*ādibuddha*) or the Great Buddha (*mahābuddha*) and depict him in sculpture and painting. According to the attributes which appear to them as most important in the Primordial Buddha, they confer his status upon Vajrasattva (= Vajradhara), Vairocana, or Akṣobhya.

[23] At least in the fully developed doctrine of the Three Bodies. The archaic form of this teaching assumes an individual Dharmakāya for each Buddha.

Amitābha, Jap: Amida (after a Japanese sculpture of the 13th century). His right hand is raised in the gesture of granting protection, his left lowered in the gesture of granting a boon. The index finger which is bent indicates the rest of self-effort required of the believer. The style of Japanese Buddhist art shows Graeco-Buddhist influences.

Although the Dharmakāya, free from all accidentals, is intelligible only to the enlightened, even less perfected beings may experience it. Depending on their degree of perfection, they perceive it in its subtle form as Sambhogakāya or in its gross appearance as Nirmāṇakāya. The Sūtras couple these two Kāyas under the term of form-body (*rūpakāya*).

II. *Sambhogakāya*

Under the designation 'Sambhogakāya', 'Body of Bliss', which has never been satisfactorily interpreted, the Mahāyāna summarises the Transcendent Buddhas. Transcendent means that they cannot be perceived by the senses, but only experienced spiritually. As this presupposes that the salvation seeker has developed the necessary mental powers, they are not visible to the ordinary worldling, but only to the advanced Bodhisattva who beholds them with his spiritual eye as radiating beings.

Intellectual Mahāyānins often understand the Sambhogakāya-Buddhas psychologically as mental creations, as ideations of

Vairocana (after a Korean sculpture of the 7th/8th century). The index finger of the right hand symbolises the one Absolute, which is encompassed by the multitude (of the fingers of the left hand). Korean art as well is influenced by Gandhāra art.

the Bodhisattvas: to the Bodhisattva his ideal becomes so vivid and alive that it takes shape as a subjective reality. Created in the experience of the Absolute, the Transcendent Buddhas are held to be manifestations of the Absolute and therefore of a higher degree of reality than the objects of the material world.

Certain Sūtras indeed contain passages which suggest this interpretation; in the Tantrayāna it even becomes the standard view. Yet it is beyond doubt that the majority of the Asian Mahāyāna adherents regard the Transcendent Buddhas as objectively existing, supramundane and subtle beings. Popular belief sees in them godlike heavenly beings to whom one can pray for rebirth in a paradise.

Likewise divergent are the opinions on the past of these Buddhas. In the Sūtras they are occasionally looked at as eternal beings who were always in existence and never had to climb the ladder to liberation. More widespread, however—and in the Buddhist system more logical—is the view that in the distant past they have worked their way up to Buddhahood. Several pre-existential biographies of Transcendent Buddhas are contained in the Sūtras.

By far the most popular Transcendent Buddha is Amitābha

Ratnasambhava (after a Nepālese hanging scroll). The right hand is in the gesture of granting a boon, the left in that of meditation. The left hand holds the wish-fulfilling jewel Cintāmaṇi which due to its transparency is invisible.

(*He of Immeasurable Radiance*) who is also called Amitāyus (*He of Immeasurable Life-span*) and, in East Asia, Amida. In a past life he is said to have taken forty-six vows by which he bound himself to lead all beings who once would remember him as a Buddha, to rebirth in the 'Pure Land' Sukhāvatī. Other highly venerated Transcendent Buddhas are Vairocana (*The Sun-like One*), Akṣobhya (*The Unshakable*), Ratnasambhava (*The Jewel-born*), Amoghasiddhi (*He of Unfailing Magical Power*) and Vajrasattva (*Whose Nature is the Vajra*) or Vajradhara (*Bearer of the Vajra*). The Sūtras mention a great number of Transcendent Buddhas, the *Saddharmapuṇḍarīka* alone enumerates twenty-three. Theoretically they are as numerous as 'grains of sand on the banks of the Ganges'.

The Transcendent Buddhas assist the deliverance of beings in three ways. Firstly, they are the teachers of the Bodhisattvas. From time to time they gather around themselves Bodhisattvas and disciples to whom they then expound the basic identity of Saṃsāra and Nirvāṇa. Secondly, they are the lords of the various paradises, in which many believers long to be reborn. The most splendid of these is that of the Buddha Amitābha. And thirdly, they are the spiritual fathers of the Nirmāṇakāya or Earthly Buddhas, whom they, out of compassion for all beings, project into the world by their meditation (*dhyāna*).[24]

III. *Nirmāṇakāya*

To the Nirmāṇakāya belong all those Buddhas who, like the historical Buddha Gautama, appear in the world in physical shape. They are called *nirmāṇa*, 'manifest beings', because of their gross nature. According to another interpretation *nirmāṇa* means '(magical) creation' and expresses that in the Mahāyāna the Earthly Buddhas are considered meditative projections of the Transcendent Buddhas. The same is meant by the *Laṅkāvatāra-sūtra* when it speaks of them as 'the body consisting of thought' (*manomayakāya*).

As persons of flesh and blood the Nirmāṇakaya-Buddhas are as much subject to the misery of ageing, illness and death as the ordinary beings of the world. From these, however, they are distinguished by thirty-two bodily characteristics and some supernatural abilities, among these the Divine Eye and the Divine Hearing, by which they can perceive what is hidden.

The function of the Earthly Buddhas is to expound the Dharma, the formulated truth, in the world. They are teachers, guide-posts to liberation but without the power to shorten the seeker's way thereto. Since moreover they are extinguished as individuals when they die prayer to them is useless except that thinking of them purifies the heart and effects a wholesome inner disposition.

In the history of the Mahāyāna several attempts have been made to schematise the doctrine of the Three Bodies by the insertion of names. The catalogue most frequently mentioned was compiled in the third or fourth century A.D. in the Vajrayāna school which belongs to the Tantrayāna branch of Buddhism. In this system which around 750 A.D. gained wide recognition in the Mahāyāna as well, the One Dharmakāya which is common to all beings, holds the top position. Underneath

[24] Hence the older secondary literature usually styles the Transcendent Buddhas as 'Dhyānibuddhas', 'Meditating Buddhas'. In the Indian texts this expression is not verifiable.

Dharmakāya	Thusness (impersonal) or Primeval Buddha (personal)				
Sambhogakāya (Transcendent Buddhas)	Vairocana	Akṣobhya	Ratnasambhava	Amitābha	Amoghasiddhi
Nirmāṇakāya (Earthly Buddhas)	Krakucchanda	Kanakamuni	Kāśyapa	Gautama	Maitreya
Transcendent Bodhisattvas	Samantabhadra	Vajrapāṇi	Ratnapāṇi	Avalokiteśvara	Viśvapāṇi

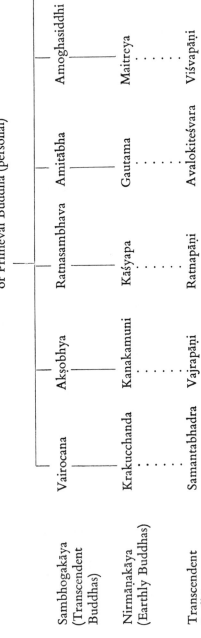

it are Five Transcendent Buddhas to each of whom an Earthly Buddha and, as a helper-in-need for the world, a Transcendent Bodhisattva are assigned (see chart, p. 108).

Some names frequently mentioned in the Sūtras are missing in this system; others which appear in it have subordinate positions in the texts. Furthermore, the assignment of only one Bodhisattva to each of the Five Buddhas is not convincing since the number of Bodhisattvas is unlimited. But in spite of these objections the system is useful as it elucidates the structure of the doctrine of the Three Bodies. Without having understood this there is no access to the Mahāyāna, for it is this system which enables the texts to describe the Buddhas as active as well as aloof from action—according to whether the passage speaks of the Earthly or the Transcendent Buddhas. The jumping between the levels allows statements which in their (apparent) paradoxity are unintelligible to the uninitiated.

Zen- (Chinese: Ch'an-) Buddhism (from the sixth century A.D. onwards in China) reinterprets the doctrine of the Three Bodies in an interesting way. It assumes that *all* beings partake in all the Three Bodies. Everyone is Nirmāṇakāya in so far as he owns a body, Sambhogakāya, inasmuch as he has freed himself from worldly fetters and Dharmakāya, in so far as he is identical with the Absolute.

3. THE BODHISATTVAS

'Bodhisattva' is the name which the Mahāyāna supplies to those beings (*sattva*) who strive systematically for enlightenment (*bodhi*), that is Buddhahood,[25] or who have already obtained it but postpone their own Static, that is Post-mortal Nirvāṇa

[25] The distinction: Buddha = self-finder of deliverance, saint (*arahant*) = one who has attained deliverance through instruction (see above, p. 79), is abandoned in many Mahāyāna texts. According to the Mahāyāna everyone has reached Buddhahood who has become spiritually similar to a Buddha, regardless of how he realised this goal. Some Mahāyāna scriptures employ the expression even more liberally by equating the terms Buddhahood and Absolute. As everyone partakes in the Absolute, even though generally unaware, he already possesses (latent) Buddhahood before his enlightenment.

(*parinirvāṇa*) until *all* beings are liberated. Bodhisattvas live exclusively for others. Their attitude is directed by mercifulness or compassion (*karuṇā*), the wish, without self-interest, to make others happy:

> How no action is appropriate for the Bodhisattvas if it does not (benefit) others, . . . is elaborated in the noble *Dharmasaṅgītisūtra.* Whatever deed the Bodhisattvas (perform, be it) with the body, voice (or) mind, all that they do for (the benefit of) others, (solely) governed by the Great Compassion for all beings; (all this) has as its cause the realisation of the welfare of beings and originates from the fervent wish for the well-being and happiness of them all. (Śs 5 p. 66)

It is the deepest conviction of the Bodhisattva that there is no difference in essence between himself and all others. It is by his belief in the essential identity of all beings (*sattvasamatā*) and by his compassion that he can be recognised as a Bodhisattva.

Whereas the Earthly Buddhas, whose task in the world is to expound the Dharma, can only help the unliberated by giving them instruction, the Bodhisattvas actively intervene in the world and willingly take the suffering of all beings onto their own shoulders. The Bodhisattva solemnly vows:

> I take the burden of suffering on myself, I am determined (to do so), I endure it . . . And why? At all cost I must (lift) the burden (of suffering) of all beings. The reason (for this resolve) is not that I find pleasure in that. (Rather) I have (heard) the supplication of all beings for rescue . . . I am resolved to abide in all the states of woe for uncounted ten millions of world-ages . . . It is better that I alone be (burdened) with suffering than that all these beings should fall into worlds of woe. (Śs 16 p. 148)

To the same extent that the Bodhisattva voluntarily takes the suffering of the world upon himself, he sacrifices his bodily, material and karmic possessions if by so doing he can bring a being closer to liberation:

> My bodies (in all rebirths) as well as all the property and pleasures which I have acquired (and will acquire) in the Three Times (past, present and future), I give away indifferently for the welfare of all beings. (3, 10)
> Nirvāṇa is the abandonment of everything, and Nirvāṇa is the goal of my thinking. As I have to abandon everything, it is better to give it to the beings. (3, 11)
> The (karmic) good which (arises) for me from reflecting on (how to make all beings) enter the Way to Enlightenment, through this (karmic good) may all beings (gain) the ornament of the Way to Enlightenment. (10, 1)
> As many (beings) in all regions of the world as are suffering from illnesses of body and mind, may they (all) obtain through my (karmic) merit oceans of happiness and joy. (10, 2)
> Whatever suffering there is in the world, may this ripen in me. May the world become happy through all the (karmic) good of the Bodhisattvas. (10, 56) (Bca pp. 17; 131; 138)

The view that karmic merit is transferable to other persons distinguishes Mahāyānic from Hīnayānic texts.

Does the Bodhisattva by dedicating (*pariṇāmanā*) his karmic merit to others not run risk of losing his position as a Bodhisattva? The question is answered in the negative, for the selfless, compassionate giving away of karmic treasures to those in need simultaneously yields him good *karman* though he is not aiming at this. His store of karmic merit is thus inexhaustible.

Yet the Bodhisattva has to check his self-offering. Alluding to stories in the Sūtras which in their description of the readiness of the Bodhisattva to sacrifice himself go beyond reasonable bounds Śāntideva says (Śs 2 V 5 p. 23) that a Bodhisattva has to be a benefactor to all and hence ought not to sacrifice his body and person for an insignificant cause. The *Prajñāpāramitā* texts stress that the Bodhisattva has to control his compassion by wisdom (*prajñā*). Compassion regulates his relationship with beings, wisdom that with the Absolute.

To what extent a Bodhisattva stands in need of wisdom is also shown by the necessity to decide what kind of help a being requires. The medicine a patient asks for is not always the right one. Real help has, therefore, often to assume the form of severity.

How should a Bodhisattva react if someone expects his assistance through an ethically objectionable deed? Should he refuse to help or should he commit the offence?

The *Upāyakauśalyasūtra*, quoted by Śāntideva, chooses the latter alternative:

> When a Bodhisattva plants the root of merit in a being in such a way that he (himself thereby) falls into misfortune . . . (and) will be cooked in hell for a hundred thousand world-ages, (in this case) . . . the Bodhisattva has patiently to take upon himself the misfortune and the torments of that hell (but) must not throw away the (kammic) good of that one being. (Śs 8 p. 93)

As this notion can easily be misused to justify reprehensible actions, it is not shared by all Mahāyānins. It does, however, demonstrate how much higher than mere formal ethics Buddhism values the ideal of compassion.

Two types of Bodhisattvas can be distinguished: Earthly and Transcendent ones. The former are human beings like millions of others, recognisable as Bodhisattvas only by their all-embracing compassion and their determination to strive first and foremost for the salvation of others and not to think of their own good. Everybody one meets may be a Bodhisattva. Without grumbling, patiently and ready for any sacrifice the Earthly Bodhisattvas accept rebirth after rebirth, for this enables them to remain close to suffering beings.

Transcendent Bodhisattvas are those who through the realisation of Six Perfections (*pāramitā*) have attained the liberating wisdom (*prajñā*) and thus sainthood from which there is no relapse. At the moment of their death they refuse to enter the Post-mortal, Perfect or Static Nirvāṇa which would make

Avalokiteśvara, with two arms as Padmapāṇi (Lotus bearer). His jewellery and five-pointed crown mark him as a transcendent being. His right hand is lowered in the gesture of granting wishes and gifts, his left hand holds the stalk of the lotus (hidden by the arm). (After a Nepālese bronze of the 13th/14th century.)

them ineffective to the world, but accept instead the 'Nirvāṇa without Standstill' or 'Active Nirvāṇa', a state of deliverance from which in their compassion they can continue to work for the benefit of the world. No longer are they perceptible through the sense-organs; since gross accidentals have largely fallen off from them they are visible only to the spiritual eye. They still act in the sphere of Saṃsāra; the saṃsāric laws, however, rebound from them. The technical term in the texts for the Transcendent Bodhisattvas is 'Great Beings' (*mahāsattva*). To give expression to their superiority over the saṃsāric world Buddhist art depicts them adorned with princely jewellery and wearing a five-pointed crown.

In their possibilities to promote the liberation of others the Transcendent Bodhisattvas far surpass the Earthly Bodhisattvas. Unlike the latter, they are no longer subject to the drudgery of rebirth but can, at their free discretion, assume any bodily form and appearance which is appropriate for the help they intend to give:

Avalokiteśvara, four-armed form. The folded inner pair of hands contains the wish-fulfilling jewel Cintāmaṇi, the outer hands hold the rosary with 108 beads and the lotus. (After a Tibetan bronze, probably of the 17th century.)

> At one moment wise Bodhisattvas show themselves in the shape of all beings and with the voices and sounds which these utter.
> They become (as circumstances require) old and ill (or) show themselves as dead; to make beings mature (for enlightenment) they play (this) illusory reality (*māyādharma*).
> Well-considered, they become courtesans to attract men. Having allured them with the hook of desire, they establish (in them) the Buddha-knowledge.
> In order to do good to beings they time and again become villagers, caravan leaders, priests, chief ministers and ministers. (Śs 18 pp. 172 + 3)

Among the many Transcendent Bodhisattvas of the Sūtras some are individualised by their exterior, their character and their office and enjoy particular veneration by the Mahāyānins.

The most important of them all is Avalokiteśvara (*The Lord who (graciously) looks down*), Padmapāṇi (*He who holds the Lotus*) or Lokeśvara (*Lord of the World*). Of him are known over 130 iconographic forms differing in the number of heads and arms, in their attributes and postures. In his headdress he often wears

Oṃ maṇipadme hūṃ—here reproduced in Tibetan script—is the mantra of Avalokiteśvara.

a small picture of the Transcendent Buddha Amitābha to whom he is assigned in the system of the Three Bodies (see above, p. 125). Some Mahāyānins regard him as a mental creation of Amitābha—a view which is hardly compatible with the assertion that the Transcendent Bodhisattvas have attained their rank through the realisation of the Six Perfections.

Avalokiteśvara's outstanding characteristic is the virtue of compassion. In order to rescue beings from suffering he is said to descend into the deepest hell. He is invoked by the famous mantra *Oṃ maṇipadme hūṃ*—'Oṃ. Jewel in the Lotus! Hūm' —which refers either to the Absolute that is contained in everything, or to the wish-fulfilling jewel which Avalokiteśvara keeps in the hollow of his hands, held palms together, in the form of a lotus bud.

Mañjuśrī (*He of Sweet Beauty*) or Mañjughosa (*The Sweet-Voiced One*) is the name of that Bodhisattva whose special task is the destruction of ignorance and the awakening of knowledge. The symbols of his function are a flaming sword in his right hand and the book of the Transcendent Wisdom on his left side. He is the lord of wisdom and the patron Bodhisattva of scholars.

Vajrapāṇi (*He who holds the Vajra*) is considered the destroyer of evil. With his Vajra, or thunderbolt sceptre, he burns to ashes all temptations barring the way of the faithful.

Mañjuśrī. With his sword which is at the same time a torch he destroys ignorance and brings knowledge. The palm-leaf book on the lotus is the Prajñāpāramitā. (After a Tibetan scroll.)

Kṣitigarbha (*He who has the Earth for his Matrix*) is the Bodhisattva who is the guardian over the hells. He continuously endeavours to ease the beings there from the effects of their bad *karman*.

The Bodhisattva Mahāsthāmaprāpta (*He who has gained great Power*) is the one who opens man's eyes to see the need for liberation. In East Asia he is often depicted together with Avalokiteśvara at the side of Amitābha. Avalokiteśvara then symbolises Amitābha's compassion and Mahāsthāmaprāpta his wisdom.

The protector of those who preach the Buddha's doctrine is Samantabhadra (*He who is all round blissful*).

Maitreya (*The Kind One*) is the Bodhisattva who at present in the Tuṣita heaven is preparing for his role as the future Buddha. In days to come he will set up on earth a realm free from suffering and restore to its old splendour the teaching of the Buddha which by then may be defiled. In a small bottle he keeps ready the elixir of deathlessness (i.e. Nirvāṇa). As the future saviour he enjoys a cult of his own with some Mahāyāna groups.

Legends are told of all these Bodhisattvas which illustrate the compassion and readiness of these helpers-in-need. Some other Transcendent Bodhisattvas, who are mentioned in the Sūtras, have no defined office or function.

The thinking of a Bodhisattva takes place on two levels. In his infinite compassion he stands up for the beings—thereby proving that he regards them as real and requiring help. But at the same time he is, as a sage, conscious of the non-existence of a Self and of the fact that all beings are mere phenomenal realities. In the highest sense there is neither suffering nor are there beings who must be liberated. A Bodhisattva has to cultivate the thought:

> I have to lead all beings (in the empirical sense) to the Post-mortal sphere of Nirvāṇa, to Perfect Extinction. And yet, after the beings have been led to Perfect Extinction, no *being* (in the absolute sense) is totally extinct.
>
> (VP 17a p. 47 ≈ VP 3)

That the suffering which the Bodhisattva takes upon himself for the benefit of others is nothing real, in no way minimises the thankfulness of the believer. For him who is enthralled in Egohood and regards the empirical world as real, suffering is real suffering, and the Bodhisattva who takes it from him deserves his gratitude.

The Mahāyānic Ways to Liberation and Nirvāṇa

1. ALL EXISTENCE IS SUFFERING

As in the Hīnayāna so in the Mahāyāna, too, existence is regarded as sorrowful. In all forms of being there are grief and pain, longing and disappointment. Life may for a time appear happy and things one has grown fond of seem lasting, but what is loved has to perish as well as the person loving it. Parting and suffering are unavoidable.

Existence is suffering (*duḥkha*) also in the philosophical sense of this word. All being lies within the sphere of rebirths (*saṃsāra*), of non-liberation, a fact which most people, however, are unable to realise. Due to their ignorance they feel so much at home in their ephemeral existence that they have no inclination to search for their true nature, the Dharmakāya, that is the Absolute which is free from suffering. Unaware of their essential liberatedness they remain bound to *saṃsāra*.

They fare like the young man whose story is related in a Chinese Sūtra. While on a journey, far away from his home he found himself through ignorance in extreme financial straits. In case of emergency his parents had sewn a jewel into the seam of his garment—but had failed to tell him of it.

Ignorance (*avidyā*, *ajñāna*) and craving (*tṛṣṇā*) are also in Mahāyānic view the causes of rebirth. They are the propelling forces which after death lead to rebirth into a new form of existence and hence to new suffering:

> (Beings) . . . are caught in the net of craving, tied by the fetter of ignorance, yoked by the craving for becoming, bound for destruction, cast into the cage of suffering, (and) heading for the prison (of worldly life). (Śs 16 p. 148)

While the Hīnayāna knows only one Way to liberation, namely that of self-discipline, the Mahāyāna teaches deliverance through Wisdom as well; through the help of Bodhisattvas; through the assistance of Transcendent Buddhas; and by cult. The Hīnayānic method of self-liberation becomes in Mahāyāna complemented by the method of 'deliverance with help from outside', or 'liberation through other-power'.

2. THE WAY OF SELF-DISCIPLINE

The Way of deliverance by self-discipline corresponds with the Eightfold Way of the Hīnayāna:

(1) Right View (*samyag-dṛṣṭi*)
(2) Right Resolve (*samyak-saṃkalpa*)
(3) Right Speech (*samyag-vāc*)
(4) Right Conduct (*samyak-karmānta*)
(5) Right Livelihood (*samyag-ājīva*)
(6) Right Effort (*samyag-vyāyāma*)
(7) Right Awareness (*samyak-smṛti*)
(8) Right Meditation (*samyak-samādhi*).

This Eightfold Way is effective for liberation by its use of the law of Karman. Every being has to expect that form of rebirth which he earns through his action-intentions in his present life. Wholesome action-intentions, that is those which conform to the Eightfold Way, lead to a rebirth closer to liberation, while unwholesome action-intentions lead away from liberation. The chance to rise from the most wretched to the highest form of existence (which, however, is still not totally free from suffering) lies in everybody's hands. Some time or other he will obtain a rebirth of such quality that he is able to walk the Eightfold Way to its end, to overcome ignorance and craving and to realise freedom from suffering, Nirvāṇa.

Although all Mahāyānic schools pretend to recognise the Eightfold Way, they have considerable doubts about it. Only the specially gifted are able to follow it, they say, whereas for all others it is too steep. Moreover, they regard it as a way for egoists who only care for their own liberation and close their eyes to the suffering of others. Lastly, they resent the purposiveness with which the Eightfold Way is often pursued.

Genuine moral discipline is unintentional and not practised for karmic merit.

> A gift . . . should not be made by a Bodhisattva who pursues a purpose (when giving). . . . (But) he who . . . makes a gift free from purpose, his stock of merit is not easily to be measured. (VP 4 p. 29)

Unintentionalness, that is freedom from craving for karmic merit, is the precondition of liberation which consists just in being free from craving and karmic bondage.

The philosophical Mahāyāna schools go even deeper in their criticism. Their objections are based on the conviction that suffering belongs to the phenomenal realm and that all beings, to the extent that they are identical with the Absolute, have always been free, though without knowing it. Liberation is, therefore, to be achieved by the removal of this ignorance and by the realisation of the Absolute; to reach deliverance is not possible by mere ethical action of which the karmic effects remain confined to the illusory world. Like other Mahāyānic thinkers, Bhāvaviveka, a monk who lived about 600 A.D. and was a follower of the Madhyamaka school, no longer understands the Eight Precepts literally, but as key-words for emancipating *insights*:

(1) Right View is insight into the Dharmakāya of the Perfect One;
(2) Right Resolve is the pacification of all imaginations;
(3) Right Speech is the realisation that language confronted with the Dharmas falls silent;
(4) Right Conduct is abstinence from any action (aiming at karmic merit);
(5) Right Livelihood consists of the insight that all Dharmas are without origination and destruction (as in the teaching of the Sarvāstivāda school);
(6) Right Effort means relinquishing Energy and Method (to obtain deliverance; that is to become intentionless) in the knowledge that no (Non-conditioned) Dharmas

(which constitute the state of deliverance) rise out of action;

(7) Right Awareness means to stop brooding over being and non-being;

(8) Right Meditation means freedom from opinions by non-grasping of Dharmas (here = ideas).

'If one views it thus in the right manner', writes Bhāvaviveka in his Śāstra *Karatalaratna* (p. 98), 'then one practises the Eightfold Way'.

3. THE WAY OF WISDOM

By knowledge (*jñāna*) the Mahāyāna understands familiarity with the doctrinal contents of the Hīnayāna. The core of these teachings are the denial of a Self (*ātman*) in the Five Groups (*skandha*) which combined constitute the empirical person, and the theory of rebirth according to the quality of karman, without a transmigrating Soul. The consciousness of a dying being occasions in a mother's womb the origination of a new empirical person without entering into this person. The propelling forces causing the consciousness to do this are craving and ignorance. Their annihilation leads to Nirvāṇa.

The basis of the Mahāyānic doctrine of rebirth is the dharma theory (see above, pp. 86 ff.) which was adopted from the later Hīnayāna and is, in many Mahāyāna texts, presupposed to be known to the reader.

This theory asserts that there are two kinds of Dharmas, Non-conditioned (*asaṃskṛta*) and Conditioned (*saṃskṛta*) ones. The Non-conditioned Dharmas are not dependent on anything, not influenced by karman and devoid of impermanence. They constitute Nirvāṇa.

The group of Conditioned Dharmas is by far the larger one. Conditioned Dharmas are those which in combination compose the empirical person. They originate conditionally from a previous Dharma combination, i.e. an individual, and by virtue of this individual's karman they amalgamate to form the new person which, after the dissolution of the older one, steps into being as his rebirth. All Conditioned Dharmas are transitory and without substratum, otherwise they could play no part in this process. There is no bearer of the Dharmas, for whatever could be considered as such, would itself be composed of Dharmas.

Even during the life-span of a being his Dharmas are not lasting but in a process of continuous disintegration, renewal and rearrangement. This explains the pulsating life processes as well as the incessant changing of the contents of the mind. Of all Conditioned Dharmas those constituting consciousness and thinking have the shortest duration. They barely exist for a split-second before they yield place to new Dharmas. And as the Dharmas constituting our mind are also decisive for our personal image of the world, the Dharma theory is also an explanation for the universe. We ourselves and our environments *are* not but *happen*. Both are processes formed of fluctuating Dharmas.

Man is comparable to a melody. No single sound or chord possesses duration and emotional value, but the continuous succession of sounds produces the phenomenon of a melody. And as a dissonance in the melody does not necessarily mean the end of the music, so the death of a being does not necessarily mean the end of the chain of Conditioned Dharmas. In most cases the Nexus of Conditioned Origination will continue after the person's death. Death itself is only a Dharma of the chain—just as dissonance is an element of the melody.

The simile explains one thing more. The audience is enchanted by the melody only as long as they perceive it as an ensouled pattern of sounds. The very moment they become aware of the separate tones, the enchantment collapses. In a similar way people are impressed by the world only as long as they regard it as something essential. When one day they see through themselves and the empirical world as phenomena produced by Conditioned Dharmas it dawns on them that from time immemorial they have been frightened by something illusory. It is this realisation which leads from knowledge to wisdom:

Prajñāpāramitā, the (female) Bodhisattva of Transcendent Wisdom (after a Javanese sculpture of the 13th century). Her hands are raised in the gesture of teaching; on the lotus to her left is the book of the Prajñāpāramitā. As Transcendent Wisdom makes up the Buddha, she is often styled 'the mother of all Buddhas'.

> Through the perception of all Dharmas . . . the deathless Nirvāṇa is recognised. (SP 5, 64 p. 100)

Whereas knowledge (*jñāna*) moves in the finite and is limited to the sphere of phenomena, wisdom (*prajñā*) reaches beyond that into the infinite and the essence. It has for its subject Absolute Reality (= Thusness = Buddhahood) which, being boundless, cannot be comprehended with the intellect: thought has no access to wisdom (AP 8 p. 96). Knowledge is a matter of the mere intellect which can grasp only fragments of reality; wisdom on the other hand is intuitive identification with the reality of all existence and being—an experience which is made with the whole of the personality after all rational limitations, views and doctrines have been discarded. It is defined as 'omniscience' (*sarvajñatā*) and in the Mahāyāna is synonymous with 'enlightenment' (*bodhi*).

The difference between knowledge and wisdom becomes evident in the scriptures of the *Prajñāpāramitā*, the 'Transcendent

Wisdom' or 'Perfection of Wisdom'. Assertions can only be made about things that are describable in words; the *Prajñāpāramitā-Sūtras*, however, try to evoke a feeling for the Absolute. Their language, therefore, oscillates between affirmation and negation. The affirmations refer to the sphere of experience, for all things we perceive are empirically existent. The negations refer to the same things in comparison with the Absolute, for measured against this they are illusion (*māyā*) and void. When the *Prajñāpāramitā* texts in the same breath affirm and deny a thing they do not thereby intend to describe it, but to convey to the reader or listener the liberating knowledge of the Illusory and the Absolute. Due to this pedagogical method they make rather confusing reading for the unprepared student.

What are the teachings of the *Prajñāpāramitās*? What do they mean by Wisdom?

Their philosophical starting point is the doctrine of the non-selfness of the person which is common to all Buddhist schools. For the term non-selfness, they introduce the more manipulatable term 'emptiness' (*śūnyatā*) which, by its ambivalence, makes all the following considerations possible. Devoid of a Self or Soul, in other words 'empty', are not only the beings but also the Conditioned (*saṃskṛta*) Dharmas or factors of existence which through their changing combinations compose beings and their world. The nature of the Conditioned Dharmas is emptiness.

The same holds true for the Non-conditioned (*asaṃskṛta*) Dharmas which represent liberation, i.e. Nirvāṇa. They, too, have no Self and are essentially empty.

From the fact that the quality of emptiness is common to both Conditioned and Non-conditioned Dharmas the wisdom-school draws two conclusions which for the Mahāyāna are of extraordinary significance:

1. Emptiness as the common quality in all opposites is their final reality: The Absolute;
2. between Saṃsāra and Nirvāṇa there is a difference only in the sphere of the illusory but not in essence.

(1) That Emptiness is the Absolute is proved by the fact that

अ

Not only in the volume of its sacred literature is Buddhism leading among the religions of the world, it is also unbeatable in the conciseness of some of its texts. Reproduced here (in the Indian *devanāgarī* script) is the 'Prajñāpāramitā in one Letter', namely a.

A is not only the first sound of the Indian alphabets and in this respect the beginning of all spoken and written knowledge, it is also, in Pāli and Sanskrit, the prefix by which affirmative notions, which according to the Prajñāpāramitā texts are but words for things illusory, are negated. By denying the essentiality of appearances it becomes itself the symbol of the essential, of absolute Emptiness.

it possesses all the characteristics of the Absolute. It is non-originated, independent of conditions, immutable, imperishable and all-comprising. It is neither non-being which would be ineffective, nor being which would be destructible. It would be wrong to understand it as an affirmative term: Emptiness, too, is empty, as the texts declare. It can neither be obtained nor abandoned, but can surely be experienced. It lies beyond our categories of thought in the realm of wisdom-experience. The all-embracing wisdom is the key to Emptiness and without Emptiness wisdom would be without content and non-existent.

Depending on what spiritual level a person stands, he gives emptiness either a positive or negative value. A person attached to the world experiences it as a constant source of suffering, for the emptiness of all things is the reason for their impermanence. Liberation to him is, at best, a paradise in which there is neither transitoriness nor suffering.

(2) The sage views emptiness in a different way. Realising that everything that exists is but a product of Dharmas and consequently illusory—though empirically real as an illusory

phenomenon—he sees Emptiness as the sole reality in all appearances. At the same time he experiences it as identical with the Thusness of the world and the Buddhahood of the Buddhas. In Emptiness as their essence he recognises the beings and the Buddhas to be one and liberated. Between a Buddha and a worldling, so it dawns on him, there is no essential difference.

Only a Buddha is conscious of his Buddhahood; he *knows* that he is a Buddha. The worldling, on the other hand, lives in ignorance of his innate Buddha-nature, suffers by attributing significance to illusory phenomena, and hence considers himself not to be liberated.

The wisdom-realisation of Emptiness radically alters the attitude of a person. Not only does he see through the saṃsāric suffering as illusion and dream, but even Buddhahood and Nirvāṇa lose their significance to him. They are illusory ideals, set up for, and useful only to, that seeker who is unaware of his essential liberatedness. Thus the monk Subhūti points out to the gods:

> *Subhūti:* Like an illusion (*māyā*) . . . are (all) beings, . . . like a dream. For illusion and beings are one, not distinct; dream and beings are one, not distinct. All Dharmas are . . . like an illusion, like a dream. Even the Stream-Entrant . . . , the Once-Returner . . . , the Non-Returner . . . , the Saint . . . , the Private Buddha . . . , the Perfect Buddha[26] . . . , (they are all) like an illusion, like a dream . . .
> *The gods:* Is the Perfect Buddha, noble Subhūti, as you say, also like an illusion, like a dream? . . .

[26] A *Stream-Entrant* is a person who can no longer be reborn below the human level. The *Once-Returner*, before he attains Nirvāṇa, has to undergo only one more rebirth, namely as a human being; the *Non-Returner* will only once be reborn in heaven. The *Saint* is exempt from rebirth and attains Nirvāṇa in this life.

Ranking above these 'Four Noble Persons', who owe their position to instruction in the Dharma, are the two kinds of Buddhas. A *Private Buddha* is one who has found enlightenment by himself, but does not preach the teaching. The *Perfect Buddha* is, in addition, also a teacher.

Subhūti: Even Nirvāṇa . . . is like an illusion, like a dream, so I declare; how much more so every other *dharma*!
The gods: Is Nirvāṇa as well, noble Subhūti, as you say, like an illusion, like a dream?
Subhūti: If there were an even higher *dharma* than Nirvāṇa, of it too I would say that it is like an illusion, like a dream. For illusion and Nirvāṇa are one, not distinct. (AP 2 p. 20)

How then can the follower of the Wisdom way free himself from saṃsāric attributes, from all that is illusory?

By developing wisdom, for wisdom destroys craving and ignorance, the two causes of suffering. Since craving feeds on sense-contacts it withers when sense-objects are seen through as Dharma-phenomena and as illusory; ignorance vanishes as soon as the Absolute (i.e. Emptiness) is realised. He who has rooted out both causes of suffering is no longer threatened by future rebirth.

4. THE BODHISATTVA WAY

The Ways of Self-discipline and of Wisdom presuppose in a follower self-restraint, intelligence and concentration power—abilities which, in the experience of Buddhism, are possessed by only a small portion of mankind. For the many who are untalented in these ways, the Mahāyāna therefore teaches three more methods of liberation: the Bodhisattva Way, the Way of Faith, and the Cultic Way.

On the Bodhisattva Way the seeker relies on the Great Compassion (*mahākaruṇā*) of the Bodhisattvas. To obtain the assistance of a Bodhisattva it suffices to invoke him entreatingly—a Bodhisattva never refuses help. On account of their inner perfection and their karmic merit accumulated through wholesome deeds in countless lives, the Transcendent Bodhisattvas are able to remove the unwholesome Karman of those in need and thus make possible their speedier emancipation. Their loving-kindness is stronger than the impeding Karman of the salvation seeker.

A Transcendent Bodhisattva enjoying particular popularity

Avalokiteśvara with eleven heads and thousand arms. Legend has it that at the sight of the suffering in the hells his head burst into ten pieces out of sheer horror. The Transcendent Buddha Amitābha, his spiritual father, then transformed each fragment into a complete head and placed an image of his own head on top of them.

Each one of Avalokiteśvara's thousand hands has an eye on its palm so that the Bodhisattva can always survey all quarters of the universe and immediately rush to the rescue when invoked. The central pair of hands holds the jewel which fulfils all wishes. Other hands bear the lotus (= purity), arrow and bow (against the temptations), the vessel with the ambrosia of deathlessness (= Nirvāṇa), the wheel of the doctrine, and the rosary of 108 pearls. The other hands are opened outwardly in the gesture of granting a wish. (Tibetan wood-cut.)

as a helper to salvation is Avalokiteśvara. He is invoked mainly in moments of acute danger, for example during a storm at sea or while crossing a perilous desert, but he can also lead to Nirvāṇa:

> Listen, you sons of noble family. The Bodhisattva Mahāsattva Avalokiteśvara is a lamp unto the blind, a parasol for those being burned by the sun's fire, a river unto the thirsting ones; he brings security to those who are in fear and terror; he is a physician to those tormented by illness; to unhappy beings he is mother and father; to those in hell he points out Nirvāṇa . . . Happy are those beings in the world, who remember his name: they are the first ones to escape saṃsāric suffering. (Kv I 16 p. 282)

The Parinibbāna *stūpa* at Kusinārā (today: Kasia). At the age of eighty the Buddha entered here into Postmortal Extinction. The ruins of the monasteries date from the 3rd to the 12th century. In the 4th century the buildings were, apparently, temporarily destroyed by fire: The Chinese travellers Fa-hsien (5th century) and Hsuan-tsang (7th century) found them abandoned. The present-day *stūpa* and the temple, which holds a reclining Buddha, are reconstructions of the 20th century on top of ruins of the Gupta period.

The cremation *stūpa* lies at a distance of approximately one and a half km from the Parinibbāna *stūpa* and marks the place of Gotama's cremation. Here also the distribution of the relics took place. Treasure-hunters have caused the upper part of the *stūpa* to cave in.
In the foreground is a modern animistic place of worship.

The mere hearing of Avalokiteśvara's name emancipates:

> So many hundred thousand millions and milliards of beings here (in the world) endure suffering—when they hear the name of the Mahāsattva Bodhisattva Avalokiteśvara, they all find liberation from the mass of suffering.
>
> (SP 24 p. 289)

To seek help in distress and deliverance from suffering through the aid of the Bodhisattvas is simple but nonetheless a method which places the seeker under obligation. For would it not be a sign of egoism and ingratitude to accept the services of the Bodhisattvas without being willing to assist them in their work for the emancipation of other beings? To become a Bodhisattva *oneself*, to be of assistance to suffering beings *oneself*, that is the proper way to thank the Bodhisattvas for their help! To be liberated is the final goal but to liberate is the more urgent and nobler one.

> Is there any better settlement of obligations with (our) true friends (the Bodhisattvas), who have given (us) immeasurable assistance, than service to all beings? (119)
> When one has done (something) for those for whose benefit (the Bodhisattvas) mangle their bodies and enter the deepest hell, then, truly, one has done good. Therefore, one must always be kind to great evil-doers. (120)
> For the benefit (of those evil-doers) even my lords (the Bodhisattvas) are voluntarily ruthless against themselves. How could I be haughty towards (my) lords (and) all those (who are patronised by them) and not rather be their servant? (121) (Bca 6 p. 58)

The Bodhisattva Way being easy to follow in its passive aspect, is in its active portion the most difficult way to deliverance which Buddhism offers. It needs extraordinary selflessness to take the Bodhisattva vow and devote oneself entirely to the aid of others without thinking of one's own liberation. Whatever the Bodhisattva thinks and does is determined by compassion (*karuṇā*):

> The Bodhisattva ... need not train himself in too many virtues (*dharma*). To one virtue ... (however) the Bodhisattva has to devote himself, he has to hold it in honour (for) through it all Buddha virtues become evident. Which is this one virtue? It is Great Compassion. (Śs 16 p. 151)

Not only monks but also lay followers can become Bodhisattvas, and, for that matter, men as well as women. The way has ten stages (*bhūmi*) on each of which the Bodhisattva develops one of the so-called virtue-perfections (*pāramitā*) until, on the seventh stage, he becomes a Transcendent, and on the tenth, a Heavenly Bodhisattva.

At the beginning of the tenfold Bodhisattva Way, but as yet not part of it, stands 'thought directed to enlightenment' (*bodhicitta*). It is the precondition for entering upon that Way, and from it the Bodhisattva draws courage for the task before him.

The Ten Stages are described differently in several texts, from which the following outline is compiled.

(1) The Joyful (*pramuditā*). The believer takes the Bodhisattva vow to dedicate himself completely to the liberation of others and to postpone his own total extinction until all beings are free from suffering. Even after death he will be able to work for the salvation of other beings, as the Bodhisattva vow is a karmic force and secures his rebirth in a form of existence which allows him to continue his efforts.

Full of joy about his being on the way, the young Bodhisattva cultivates in particular the virtue-perfection of openhandedness (*dāna*). Without egoistic ulterior motives, he gives his possessions away to those in need.

(2) The Immaculate (*vimalā*). He perfects his self-discipline (*śīla*).

(3) The Radiating (*prabhākārī*). The Bodhisattva gains insight into the transient nature of the world and develops the

virtue of patience (*kṣānti*). 'Patience' here means willing endurance of adversities and perseverance in efforts for the deliverance of the world.

(4) The Blazing (*arciṣmatī*). As with flames, the Bodhisattva burns the remnant of false ideas. He cultivates will-power (*vīrya*) which he needs to be victorious in his struggle for the liberation of all beings.

(5) The Extremely Difficult to Conquer (*sudurjayā*). He perfects himself in meditation (*dhyāna*) in order to grasp intuitively the true nature of existence.

(6) The (stage) Facing (Wisdom) (*abhimukhī*). The Bodhisattva obtains insight into Conditioned Origination which is the cause of sorrowful individual existence. His wisdom (*prajñā*) or omniscience (*sarvajñatā*) becomes perfect as he realises the Emptiness of all beings and things and cognises it as the Absolute. Whereas his wisdom tells him that he himself is nothing but an illusory being in a mere phenomenal world, trying to liberate phantoms from illusory suffering, his compassion reminds him nevertheless not to slacken in his efforts to rescue those beings who believe themselves to be suffering.

From the sixth stage on which he gains wisdom (= enlightenment) and becomes a saint, the Bodhisattva would be able to enter, on death, the Static (*pratiṣṭhita*) Nirvāṇa, that is to become extinct for the world. However, if he took this chance he would not deserve the title Bodhisattva. Out of compassion for all beings he merely enters into the Active (*apratiṣṭhita*) Nirvāṇa, a state of deliverance which sets him free from samsāric compulsion but enables him to stay on in the saṃsāric world and so to continue promoting the deliverance of beings.

(7) The Far-going (*dūraṅgamā*). The Bodhisattva changes over into a new mode of being. He becomes a *Transcendent* Bodhisattva, which means that he is no longer tied to a physical body. According to the assistance he wants to give, he can of his own free will assume any conceivable appearance, if necessary several at the same time. He is now in full possession of the right method (*upāya*), has 'skill in means'. He knows

how each being according to his power of comprehension and disposition can be guided onto the way to liberation.

(8) The Immovable (*acalā*). He gains the ability of transferring his karmic merit to unliberated beings (*pariṇāmanā*). Their well-being is his vow (*praṇidhāna*).

(9) The Good-Thoughts (*sādhumatī*). With strength (*bala*) he devotes himself to the task of executing his vow to guide all beings to deliverance. A Bodhisattva of the ninth stage is, for example, Avalokiteśvara.

(10) The Cloud of the Doctrine (*dharmamegha*). The Bodhisattva has realised all knowledge (*jñāna*). His body begins to radiate and to illumine the universe. Amidst the Bodhisattvas of the Ten Directions he sits on a lotus in the Tuṣita heaven. One more change of existence and he will attain Buddhaship. Maitreya is a Bodhisattva of this tenth floor of perfection.

The Six or Ten Perfections, as the virtues of the Bodhisattva are called, also play a role outside the ten-staged Bodhisattva career and are therefore listed here again. They are:

open-handedness (*dāna*),
discipline (*śīla*),
patience (*kṣānti*),
will-power (*vīrya*),
meditation (*dyāna*), and
wisdom (*prajñā*).

These Six Perfections are said (AP 22 p. 197) to be the true friends of the Bodhisattva and the cause of his omniscience.

The other four Perfections are
(right) method (*upāya*),
vow (*praṇidhāna*),
strength (*bala*), and
knowledge (*jñāna*).

They were added in more recent times in order to assign one Perfection to each one of the Ten Stages of the Bodhisattva career. This piecing together of the catalogue explains the oddities in the succession of the Perfections.

5. THE WAY OF FAITH

Though the Bodhisattva Way is, in its passive part, an easy path to deliverance—the moral obligation to thank the Bodhisattvas for the aid they have given by becoming a Bodhisattva oneself prevents many from setting foot on it. The great mass needs more comfortable ways to liberation, ways which necessitate no exertion and which do not put them under obligation. For people of this type the Mahāyāna teaches the Way of Faith and the Cultic Way.

The word 'faith' is a somewhat insufficient translation of the term *śraddhā*. For *śraddhā* signifies no rational accepting-as-true, but faithful confidence. The word is almost synonymous with the expression *bhakti*, 'devotion', which is often employed in the later texts of the school of Faith.

To the confessors of this Way, faith is the central virtue from which all other virtues automatically develop and which unfailingly leads to rebirth in a Buddha paradise:

> Faith is the guide, mother, originator, protector, increaser of all virtues, dispeller of doubts, rescuer from the flood of rebirths. Faith is the signpost to the secure city (of the Buddha paradise).
>
> . . .
>
> Faith creates liking in renunciation, faith creates delight in the doctrine of the victors (i.e. the Buddhas), faith creates distinction in the knowledge of the virtues; it leads in the direction of the Buddha goal. (Śs 1 p. 4 f.)

In the understanding of the Mahāyāna faithful confidence is doubly effective. On the one hand it produces karmic merit (*puṇya*), whereby through its 'unimaginable' (*acintya*) result it is superior to common morals (*śīla*) whose effect can only be finite and located in the sphere of Saṃsāra. On the other hand, since it refers to a Transcendent Bodhisattva or Buddha, it is the means to invoke his compassion and help. What wholesome deeds alone can never achieve, namely to obtain the assistance of a transcendent being, can be brought about by

Amitāyus, a form of Amitābha and lord of the paradise Sukhāvatī. The vessel in his hands, which are put over one another in the meditation gesture, contains the nectar of deathlessness. (After a Tibetan bronze.)

hearing his name, thinking of him with trust and invoking him.

Śraddhā is mainly directed to two transcendent beings: the Bodhisattva Avalokiteśvara and the Buddha Amitābha or Amitāyus, called in East Asia Amida. To the former the faithful prefer to appeal when in acute distress; Amitābha, however, is more a helper to salvation. In a distant pre-existence as the monk Dharmākara he is said to have vowed to become a Buddha, provided that he could succeed in creating through his karmic merit a Pure Buddha Paradise called Sukhāvatī, 'the Happy (Land)'. In 46 vows (*praṇidhāna*) before the Buddha Lokeśvararāja, which are reproduced in the Longer *Sukhāvatīvyūhasūtra*, he made known to which actions for all beings he commits himself. The most important vows of Dharmākara (i.e. Amitābha) are (in the Sanskrit version of the Sūtra which varies from the Chinese recension) numbers 18 and 19 which state the methods of calling on Amitābha's aid in the moment of death and for gaining rebirth in his paradise.

> (18) When, O Lord, after I have obtained enlightenment, beings in other world systems through hearing my name develop a thought for the highest, Perfect Enlightenment and remember me with a clear mind—if in the moment of

Maitreya as a Bodhisattva in the Tuṣita heaven (after a sculpture of the 12th century from Viṣṇupur). The Campa blossom at his left and the stūpa in his stacked-up hair make identification possible. His right hand in the expounding gesture marks him as explaining the Dharma to the gods.

their death, after I, surrounded by a congregation of monks, have gone to them, I should not stand before them as the Venerated One in order to protect their minds from fear—then may I not obtain the highest, Perfect Enlightenment. (19) When, O Lord, after I have obtained enlightenment, beings in incalculable, numberless Buddha lands through hearing my name direct their thoughts to rebirth in (my) Buddha land (*Sukhāvatī*) and so bring to maturity the roots of (karmic) merit—if they are not reborn there in (my) Buddha land, even though they had only directed their thoughts ten times (to me and my Buddha paradise) ... —may I not then obtain the highest, Perfect Enlightenment.

(SvL 8 p. 227)

Relieved of unwholesome Karman and free from suffering (SvL 18) the follower, reborn in the paradise Sukhāvatī, here matures to wisdom (38) and Nirvāṇa (24).

According to other scriptures the *bhakta* (devotee) can be

A vision of the future: Maitreya as a Buddha (after a Tibetan bronze). The fingers of his raised right hand, in the gesture of expounding, form the wheel of the teaching, his left hand rests in the gesture of meditation.

reborn in the paradise Sukhāvatī, located in the West, as well as in the Eastern paradise Abhirati of the Buddha Akṣobhya, in the Southern paradise of the Buddha Ratnaketu, or in the Northern paradise of the Buddha Dundubhīśvara. In the distant future yet another paradise will be established on earth by the Buddha Maitreya who is at present still a Bodhisattva in the Tuṣita heaven. Unlike the historical Buddha Gautama, who sprang from the warrior caste (*kṣatriya*), the Buddha Maitreya will be born as a brahmin.

In the texts the numerous Buddha paradises are divided into two groups. For the first group there is no special collective name, but the second are the so-called 'Pure Lands'. The ordinary paradises lie within our universe and more or less resemble our world, but are free from ill-will and violence. The Pure Lands on the other hand are transcendent and their inhabitants are not born into them on account of their karmic merit, but through the grace of a Transcendent Buddha. They are radiating and lovely paradises of bliss. Amitābha's paradise Sukhāvatī is the prototype of a Pure Land. Each of these lands (*kṣetra*) is under the control and care of a Transcendent Buddha, who regards it his main task to impart liberating wisdom to the beings of his paradise.

Set against the popular notion which sees manifest realities in these paradises, is the philosophical conception according to which they are subjective mental creations. A person with powerful karmic attachment to our world ideates for himself a paradise modelled after this world; a person who is karmically freer, however, ideates for himself a Pure Land.

In whatever way a Buddha paradise may be imagined, no Sūtra explains and no knowledgeable follower regards it as the final goal of salvation. It is merely an intermediate station on the way to liberation, which even with the School of Faith involves the extinction (*nirvāṇa*) of the empirical personality. When a believer has obtained rebirth in a Buddha paradise, the faith which led him there does not help him any further: Nirvāṇa can be realised solely through Wisdom or Insight. But in order to develop these, rebirth in a Buddha land offers the best starting-point.

The teaching of the Way of Faith has given rise to the question whether a wicked man as well can obtain rebirth in a Buddha paradise. Some Mahāyānic schools deny this. Others hold that no person with faithful confidence in a Buddha can be a villain. A third group—most prominently represented by the East Asian Amida- (= Amitābha-) Buddhism—answers the question with affirmation. Amida's compassion, they say, embraces all beings, even the vilest ones. Nay, these are even nearer to salvation as they do not cherish the arrogant opinion that they could attain salvation by their own power.

6. THE CULTIC WAY

No Mahāyānin intent on the purity of his religion likes to concede that the Mahāyāna—doubtlessly as a concession to the pious masses—also approves of cult as a way to liberation. In fact the Cultic Way is the most unassuming form of Buddhism. It cannot, however, be disavowed. The religious practice in Mahāyānic countries as well as written documents give evidence of its existence.

Whereas Śāntideva (seventh century A.D.) in his anthology *Śikṣāsamuccaya* (17 p. 156 f.) only quotes Sūtra passages which regard ritual practice as instrumental to better rebirth, the *Saddharmapuṇḍarīkasūtra* (2, 78–94) characterises the worship of relics, the erection of Stūpas, the creating of Buddha images, the offering of flowers and incense, and the making of music at shrines as the way to Enlightenment. The text continues:

> Those who at a Stūpa have shown (their) veneration (by placing their palms together, either in the) perfect (way) or (only) with *one* hand, (and those who) have bent the erect head and body a single time for a moment, (95)
> —(moreover the people who) have at those relic containers (i.e. *stūpas*) said 'Honour to the Buddha!' a single time (and), be it only with distracted mind, have all obtained Supreme Enlightenment (*agrabodhi*). (96) (SP 2, 95 f. p. 39)

This means that mental attitude plays no role in the Cultic Way: even if performed 'with distracted mind' the ritual leads to liberation. Although this view contradicts the conviction of all other Buddhist Ways to emancipation which all stress the necessity of proper inner disposition, it nevertheless also inspires hope for liberation in people of weak will.

7. THE GOAL: NIRVĀṆA

For the followers of the Bodhisattva Way and the Way of Faith, Nirvāṇa has receded into the background. They have, respectively, set themselves intermediate goals: liberation of the world and rebirth in a Buddha paradise. Yet for these two schools as well, total extinction as aspired to by all Buddhist schools remains the ultimate goal.

Whereas deliverance in the Hīnayāna is only possible through Enlightenment (*bodhi*), in the Mahāyāna it is only through Enlightenment or Wisdom (*prajñā*). On the Wisdom Way declaredly, but no less on the Ways of the Bodhisattva and of Faith, Wisdom is the precondition to Nirvāṇa. Transcendent Bodhisattvaship is attained through the virtue of

Wisdom-perfection, and the Way of Faith is not immediately conducive to deliverance, but leads to rebirth in a Buddha paradise where the faithful then mature to Wisdom (= liberation). Enlightenment is also the goal of the Cultic Way.

However, so far as the content of the liberating insight is concerned, Hīnayāna and Mahāyāna differ from each other. Hīnayānic Enlightenment has for its object the Four Noble Truths—of suffering, its origin, its cessation, and the way to its cessation. Wisdom in the Mahāyānic sense, on the other hand, is the awareness that Saṃsāra and Nirvāṇa, worldly beings and Buddhas, are opposites only superficially but in essence are one with the Absolute. What distinguishes the Buddha from the worldling is his attitude towards existence. The worldling believes himself to be separated from the Buddha nature; he regards the saṃsāric process as something essential and hence suffers under its adversities. The Liberated One by contrast lives in the consciousness of his essential Buddha nature (= liberatedness) and recognises suffering as an interplay of dharmas and mere illusion. He has 'returned home' to the motionless ideal centre of the rotating wheel of Samsāra. The Four Characteristics of Nirvāṇa are: permanence (of the Absolute), bliss (in the awareness of one's identity with it), freedom (from bondage to sorrowful things), and purity (of emotions and craving).

A second difference between the Hīnayānic and the Mahāyānic conceptions of Nirvāṇa concerns the subdivision of the state of liberation into two 'spheres'. The Hīnayāna distinguishes between (i) Pre-mortal and (ii) Post-mortal Nirvāṇa, some Mahāyānic Sūtras between (a) Active and (b) Static Nirvāṇa.

(a) 'Without standstill' (*apratiṣṭhita*) or 'active' is the altruistic state of Nirvāṇa in which the Liberated One has attained saintship, but instead of becoming extinguished in death lives on as a Transcendent Bodhisattva in order to assist all beings. A Liberated One in Active Nirvāṇa is free from karmic bonds, from greed, hatred and delusion and acts without getting re-involved in Saṃsāra by his actions. The natural laws no longer bind him; he can appear at will in any place and in any conceivable form.

(b) In Static (*pratiṣṭhita*) Nirvāṇa which can be equated with (ii) Post-mortal Nirvāṇa, the Liberated One loses all individuality at the moment of death and so becomes untraceable. He has discarded everything that is not pure Absolute. Since the terms of individuality are no longer applicable to him, it is impossible to state anything about 'him'. To speak of the Liberated One in Static Nirvāṇa means to speak of the Absolute. But speaking of the Absolute is like trying to trap a scent with one's hands.

IV

PHILOSOPHICAL SCHOOLS OF THE MAHĀYĀNA

The philosophical Mahāyāna schools developed from the religious ones through systematisation and elaboration of the teachings of the Sūtras. Later on, when further Sūtras were composed, many notions defined by the Mahāyānic thinkers were incorporated into these new books so that today they can be regarded as common Mahāyānic knowledge. The Mahāyāna philosophers were originators only in the second place; above all they were interpreters and consolidators of existing ideas. Their main achievement is the new viewpoint under which they rearranged the ideas of the old texts into distinct systems, and the creation of a philosophical logic.

The philosophy of the Mahāyāna concentrates on one problem: the relationship between the Many and the One. The multiplicity of the phenomena which compose the world and the unity of the principle which is sensed in them as the Absolute and which has to be realised through individual experience—these are the poles between which Mahāyānic thinking is stretched.

The Madhyamaka (Śūnyatāvāda) System

1. THINKERS AND ŚĀSTRAS

There are two Sūtras which form the basis for the conceptions of the Madhyamaka or Śūnyatāvāda school: the *Prajñāpāramitā* and the *Saddharmapuṇḍarīka*. In addition there are several Śāstras or textbooks by thinkers known by name.

Nāgārjuna, the initiator of the Madhyamaka school, probably lived at the beginning of the second century A.D. Born into a brahmin family of Central India, he is said to have come to Buddhism through a vow. He spent one period of his life in Amarāvatī; later he resided in or near Nāgārjunakoṇḍa, where it is thought he died, probably murdered by order of a prince of the Śātavāhana dynasty. The statement that he was abbot of the monastic university of Nālandā is definitely incorrect. Nālandā university was not founded until the third century.

The following works of Nāgārjuna are preserved in Sanskrit: *Madhyamakaśāstra*, *Vigrahavyāvartaṇī*, *Ratnāvalī*, *Catuḥstava*, *Mahāyānaviṃśikā*,[27] *Dharmasaṅgraha*,[27] and *Suhṛllekha*.[27]

Other thinkers of the Madhyamaka are Āryadeva (second/third century), a direct disciple of Nāgārjuna; Buddhapālita (fifth century), Bhāvaviveka or Bhāvya (sixth/seventh century), Candrakīrti, Śāntideva (seventh century), Śāntarakṣita and Kamalaśīla (eighth century). Works by them, too, have come down to us in Sanskrit. Śāntarakṣita and his pupil Kamalaśīla, who both endeavoured to create a synthesis of the Madhyamaka system with that of the Yogācāra, have played a decisive role in introducing Buddhism into Tibet. It was Śāntarakṣita who for the first time ordained Tibetans as Buddhist monks and thus secured for the Madhyamaka school a lasting influence in the Land of Snows.

2. TEACHINGS

Nāgārjuna's works contain hardly more positive statements than the texts of the *Prajñāpāramitā* whose ideas he systematises.

[27] Authenticity doubtful.

He was concerned above all with demonstrating the untenability of any affirmative assertion and proving the inner inconsistency of all possible philosophical systems. In doing so he uses bold, occasionally even faulty,[28] logic, but the very daring of his argumentation gives his thought effectiveness and contributed to the diffusion of the Madhyamaka.

The designation Madhyamaka refers to the Middle Way (*madhyamā pratipad*) which Nāgārjuna teaches with regard to the being or non-being of all things:

> 'It is'—this is the grasping of eternity; 'it is not'—this is the view of annihilation.
> Therefore, an intelligent (person) should not be attached to either being or non-being. (Mś 15,[10])

But how, if the world is neither being nor non-being, does it exist? It exists like a fata Morgana: as a deceiving phenomenon it is real, but the thing it conjures up is an illusion (*māyā*):

> As an illusion, as similar to a dream, to a castle in the air have the origination, existence and destruction (of all things) been explained. (7, 34)

Such a statement already presupposes a philosophical measure by which one can distinguish the illusory from the real. Nāgārjuna sees this measure in 'own-beingness' (*svabhāvatā*) or 'essentiality'. Essentiality means that something is non-originated (15, 1), not dependent on anything for its existence (15, 2) and consequently eternal (15, 11). These characteristics cannot be found in the empirical world, for it is devoid of essentiality (24, 38), that is empty.

[28] e.g. Mś 3, 2: 'The eye does not perceive itself. If it does not perceive itself, how can it see other (things)?' Logical mistakes according to the pattern: 'If p, then q; if not-p, then q', can be demonstrated in the Mś twelve times, e.g. 20, 15. Even if one grants that sentences of this kind are meant as pedagogical instruments, this still does not remove their faulty logic.

Whereas Nāgārjuna uses the adjectives 'non-essential' (*asvabhāva*) and 'empty' (*śūnya*) as synonyms, he does not regard as such the nouns 'non-essentiality' (*asvabhāvatā* or *niḥsvabhāvatā*) and 'emptiness' (*śūnyatā*).

Stating the non-essentiality of a thing is always a negative judgement; stating its emptiness, however, is an ambivalent judgement. On the one hand 'emptiness' signifies the non-existence of an individual Soul or Self, on the other hand essential liberatedness. For just because there is no Soul in beings but emptiness, they are essentially liberated. The Emptiness of every being which is identical with the Emptiness of all others, possesses all the characteristics of the essence. To become aware of one's essential Emptiness is to achieve liberation. In the Madhyamaka system as in the *Prajñāpāramitā* texts Emptiness is the Absolute.

In the process of existence as well as in the process of liberation non-essentiality and Emptiness operate in three ways. They are the prerequisites for (1) the origination of all beings and (2) of suffering, but they also make possible (3) emancipation from Saṃsāra which is extinction.

(1) The world, the individual and the chain of rebirths are nothing but phenomena brought about by the Conditioned Origination and the speedy disappearance of Conditioned Dharmas. This fluctuating process would be impossible if the Dharmas as its components were essential, that is permanent entities: only non-essentiality and Emptiness make them fit to be the factors of existence. Non-essentiality (= Emptiness) is thus the precondition for the rise of suffering (24, 22).

Nāgārjuna's opponents have construed this to mean that he sees in Emptiness the *cause* of suffering or the factor producing suffering. This is a misinterpretation. Nāgārjuna also holds that Emptiness can never give rise to anything. However, the process of Conditioned Origination, urged on by craving and ignorance, takes place in Emptiness and is inconceivable without it. Emptiness is neither the primeval ground nor the cause, yet the precondition of Samsāra—the unshakable in all change.

(2) Since all Dharmas arise from conditions and hence are

empty (24, 19), the world of appearances formed by them is transient. Transitoriness, however, is suffering (24, 21).

(3) If suffering were something essential, it would never be possible to annihilate it (24, 23). Emptiness makes the termination of suffering possible (24, 39).

To the question as to what is meant by Emptiness, Nāgārjuna replies: Emptiness is Conditioned Origination (*pratītyasamutpāda*—24, 18), for

> as there is no Dharma, which did not originate from conditions,
> there is no Dharma, which is not empty. (24, 19)

Apart from the fact that this reply does not define Emptiness, but only describes it as a quality of the Dharmas, it is also incomplete. 'Emptiness' also designates, as Nāgārjuna well knew, a mental attitude: the non-attachment to theorems (13, 8). Emptiness as the Absolute and freedom is realised by means of Emptiness-*attitude*. When the mind is cleared from consent or denial, it merges with the Absolute (*tattva*). The characteristics of the Absolute are that it is not discernible by the help of others, that it is tranquil, not multiple through multiplicity, without polarity and unequivocal (18, 9). Emptiness, writes Candrakīrti (in his commentary to Mś 18, 5 p. 150), is Nirvāna.

It would be a mistake to raise Emptiness, which is the annulment of all theories, to a theory and to cling to it (13, 8). He who does so, comments Candrakīrti (p. 108), is like a person to whom a merchant has said that he has nothing to sell and who now hopes to buy this nothing and to carry it home. In the same context he quotes a simile from the *Ratnakūṭasūtra*: Emptiness is like a laxative; it serves for purgation, but the patient is only healed when the medicament has purged itself away.

It lends itself to contrasting the One Emptiness with the multiplicity composed of Conditioned Dharmas and to taking it as the Wholly-Different. Such a segregation would, however, be wrong. The Dharmas are neither isolated from each other nor in their relation to the Absolute. For since they are all empty and undifferentiated (25, 22), and their Emptiness is the Absolute, there is no difference in essence between the Dharma phenomena and the Absolute (= Nirvāṇa):

> There is no difference between Saṃsāra and Nirvāṇa;
> there is no difference between Nirvāṇa and Saṃsāra.
> The sphere of Nirvāṇa is also the sphere of Saṃsāra.
> Between these two there is not the slightest difference.
> (25, 19–20)

Happiness and suffering, I and Thou—all pairs of opposites are opposites only as appearances, opposites merely in the phenomenal sphere, but they are identical in essence, namely Emptiness which needs no liberation as it is liberation.

Nāgārjuna's definition of Nirvāṇa is as elusive as that of Emptiness. Nirvāṇa is neither attained nor abandoned, neither interrupted nor eternal, neither destroyed nor originated (25, 3). It is neither being nor non-being (25, 10). In Nirvāṇa all perception ceases, the world of multiplicity (*prapañca*) comes to rest and there reigns bliss (25, 24).

It is through Emptiness that Nirvāṇa is realised:

> The confessor of Emptiness (*śūnyatāvādin*) is not captivated by the Dharmas of the world, as he does not rely on them. When he gains something, he is not carried away; when he fails to gain something, he is not disappointed. Fame does not make him proud, no-fame does not depress him; he does not become depressed through reprimand, nor elevated through praise; he is not happy through good fortune, nor sad through sorrow. . . . For the confessor of Emptiness there is thus neither sympathy nor antipathy. (Śs p. 264)

In Nāgārjuna's own words:

> Liberation (*mokṣa*) results from the destruction of Karman

The wheel of the teaching, Mahāyānic form. The eight spokes symbolise the rules of the Eightfold Way to the termination of suffering; the symbol in the centre was adopted from China and represents the interwovenness of suffering and liberation. (Tibetan wood-cut.)

> and the defilements (*kleśa*). Karman and the defilements result from ideas.
> These from multiplicity. Multiplicity, however, is annulled in Emptiness. (Mś 18, 5)

In other words: realisation of Emptiness destroys the compulsion for rebirth. As liberation from rebirth is the goal of the Buddha's doctrine, a person has so fulfilled the teaching.

Nāgārjuna's views did not remain undisputed. His opponents argue: If everything is empty, then there are neither the Four Noble Truths of the Buddha nor a karmic reward for actions; consequently all ethical discipline is futile (Mś 24, 1–4). This objection misses the point. Although Nāgārjuna regards all things, including the Buddha's teaching, as empty, he does not deny their reality as appearances. The world is like a dream: depressingly real as long as one does not wake up.

Truth, he explains, is double or two-levelled (24, 8). In practical life we apply Relative (lit. 'veiling') Truth (*saṃvṛti satya*). It employs conventional terms like 'Karman' and 'liberation' and makes use of logical arguments, for as most people are unable to think of what is beyond the sphere of the phenomenal, they only understand this kind of language. If, however, the Emptiness of all appearances is indicated and shown as the Absolute, we must apply 'Truth in the Supreme Sense' (*paramārtha satya*) which is trans-logical. Relative Truth speaks of the difference between things, Supreme Truth of their essential identity.

Relative Truth is also used by the Bodhisattva in his endeavours to liberate all beings, for although beings are basically Emptiness and free from time immemorial, they are unaware of their freedom and hence in need of his help. Without slackening his efforts for the benefit of others, the Bodhisattva thinks for himself on two levels:

> As many beings . . . as there are . . . , all these should be led by me to perfect extinction. And yet, although countless beings have thus been led to perfect extinction, no *being* whatsoever was led to extinction. And why? If . . . a Bodhisattva holds the notion of 'being', he cannot be called a Bodhisattva. And why? He is not to be called a Bodhisattva who holds the notion 'Self' (*ātman*) or the notion 'being' or the notion 'Soul' (*jīva*) or the notion 'person' (*pudgala*).
>
> (VP 3 p. 28 f.)

The Mādhyamika must learn to live in relativity. He gives away gifts benevolently and from his heart, but accompanied by the Threefold Knowledge: insight into the phenomenal nature of his gift, the giver and the recipient.

The Yogācāra (Vijñānavāda) System

1. THINKERS AND ŚĀSTRAS

The fundamental texts of the Yogācāra or Vijñānavāda School are the *Laṅkāvatāra*-, the *Avataṃsaka*- and the *Sandhinirmocana-Sūtras* of which, however, only the first is preserved in Sanskrit. There are, moreover, a number of Śāstras which systematise the teachings of these Sūtras.

Three men have stamped the Yogācāra with their personalities: Maitreya or Maitreyanātha (third/fourth century), Asaṅga, and Vasubandhu (fourth/fifth century). Maitreya(nātha)'s historicity is questioned by some, but modern scholars tend to regard him a real person. He is believed to have been the teacher of Asaṅga. Of his works, the *Yogācārabhūmiśāstra*, *Madhyāntavibhāga*, *Mahāyānasūtrālaṅkāra*, *Abhisamayālaṅkāra* and the *Ratnagotravibhāga* survive in Sanskrit.

Asaṅga and Vasubandhu were brothers and descended from a brahmin family from Puruṣapura (now: Peshawar in Pakistan). Before their conversion to Mahāyāna they are said to have been adherents of the Sarvāstivāda School.

Asaṅga is the author of the *Dharmatāvibhaṅga* and the *Abhidharmasamuccaya*. Other works by him are handed down in translation only.

Tradition has it that Vasubandhu was converted to Mahāyāna by his brother Asaṅga after he, as a Hīnayāna follower, had written several books, among them the *Abhidharmakośa*. Recent research, however, points out that Vasubandhu, the author of the *Abhidharmakośa*, and Vasubandhu the Yogācārin are probably not identical. The most instructive works of the latter Vasubandhu are the *Trisvabhāvanirdeśa* and the *Vijñaptimātratāsiddhi*. The *Siddhi* consists of two philosophical treatises, the *Viṃśatikā* and the *Triṃśikā*.

How differently Asaṅga and Vasubandhu place the emphasis in their school is evident by the fact that they give it different names. Asaṅga, being a religious practician, particularly stresses meditation. Understanding the way to deliverance as a special type of Yoga, he calls the system Yogācāra, 'conduct in Yoga'. Vasubandhu on the other hand, being more of a theoretician and thinker, styles the system Vijñānavāda, 'consciousness doctrine', as it explains all that exists as consciousness or mind.

Other philosophers of the Yogācāra worthy to be named are: Dignāga or Dinnāga (fifth/sixth century), Sthiramati and Dharmapāla (sixth century), Candragomin, Dharmakīrti (seventh century), Dharmottara (ninth century) and Haribhadra (tenth century). Their writings deal mainly with problems of epistemology and logic.

2. TEACHINGS

According to the Yogācāra everything perceptible is only mind (*cittamātra*):

> There are no visible (things), the external world is mind (*citta*),
> merely mind is seen; body, property and environment I call but mind. (LS 3, 33 p. 154)

Sentences like 'The world is only mind' (LS 2, 136 p. 73) and 'The triple world is mind itself' (2 p. 80) can be found by the dozen in the *Laṅkāvatārasūtra*.

However, acts of perception do not take existing objects into the mind. What is generally called 'perception' is a process of imagination which *creates* in us the picture of the supposed objects. The things we believe that we see, grasp, taste and so on, are in reality ideations. Where the Madhyamaka beholds Dharmas, the Yogācāra sees only flashes of consciousness, and it is the incessant succession of these flashes which conjures up in us the impression of a world. That different people 'perceive' the same world is explained in that they are tainted with similar Karman which leads them to similar ideations. That we cannot voluntarily change the world which we ideate is ascribed to our being bound by our Karman. Without the deluding power of old, unwholesome Karman, everybody would realise that his suffering is only ideated suffering, the termination of which lies within himself.

Against those philosophical schools which take the empirical world for real, the Yogācārins substantiate their idealism in the following way: Things, they say, exist only when they are contents of our consciousness; without consciousness of them they are non-existent. Thus, since our idea of things is the only proof for their existence—would it not be sheer speculation from this mental picture of objects to conclude their autonomous existence? Things *are* consciousness, *are* mind, that is the only safe assertion one can make about them.

The theory is taken even further:

> All this is but mind. Mind makes its appearance in two ways: As (the object) to be grasped and as the grasper (i.e. the subject). There is no Self and nothing of the nature of a Self. (LS 3, 121, p. 209)

Hence, not only are objects 'mind', that is mental creations or ideations, but so is the subject. The empirical person has as little existence independent from mind as the world; the person, too, is an ideation. But which mind is the ideator?

It is obvious that the mind (*citta*) which originates the subject is not the mind of the person himself as this would mean that the individual is his own ideator. Here mind should rather be taken as something beyond the empirical person, a pre- or supra-individual principle. In fact 'mind' in the Yogācāra system is a designation of the Absolute. Thusness, Emptiness, Nirvāṇa, Essence of Reality and Mind are identical (LS 3, 31 p. 154). Now and then this Absolute is conceived as Dharmatābuddha or Dharmabuddha (e.g. LSsag 382).

How it could happen that the Absolute Mind individuates itself as an empirical person is explained in the Yogācāra by a special theory. This theory of individuation is no cosmogonic doctrine, for it presupposes the existence of old Karman. The quest for a first beginning is never a problem with which Buddhist thought is concerned.

The theory of individuation distinguishes between two layers of the mind (*citta*): the Storehouse- or Base-consciousness (*ālayavijñāna*) and the Individual-consciousnesses or Thought-consciousnesses (*manovijñāna* or *manas*). Both are in essence identical and only differ in their functions.

'Base-consciousness' is that part of the *citta* which eternally rests in itself. As the Absolute, as being in itself and immutable, it is often compared with the ocean. For as the ocean is a unity and all water in the world is derived from it, so the Base-consciousness, too, is an ocean and all existing things spring from it. In essence it is free from inconstancy and ill-will, without claim to be a Self, and pure in its nature (LS 6 p. 220 f.). And as the ocean offers a home to sundry things like fish and seaweed, so too does the Base-consciousness. It is the storehouse (*ālaya*) of karmic impressions (*vāsanā*) or karman-seeds which have been occasioned and left behind by past individuals. Drifting about in the Base-consciousness as if in a nutritive liquid, these karmic seeds ripen into thinking (*manas*) or Thought-consciousnesses (*manovijñāna*), each of which believes that it is a Self, a real physical person: They individuate themselves. The individuations again ideate each for themselves private worlds—mere fancies, but fancies in which they produce new karmic seeds which then sink into the Base-consciousness. In this cycle, which is not a physical process but takes place as a sequence of ideas in the Base-consciousness, the Yogācāra sees the wheel of rebirths.

The *Laṅkāvatārasūtra* outlines this cycle thus:

> The Thought-consciousness (*manovijñāna*) by being active through its urge to make observations in the (ideated) sense-world, interpenetrates the Base-consciousness (*ālayavijñāna*) with karmic impressions (*vāsanā*). (In the Base-consciousness from these karmic impressions) there develops thought (*manas*) which brings with it the proneness for grasping a (supposed) Self and something of the nature of Self. . . . It is (however) without the characteristic of a body (and) dependent on the Base-consciousness as its cause.
>
> (LS 2 p. 126 f.)

The same Sūtra describes the method for deliverance from this cycle:

> ... (People) who seek Nirvāṇa (because they are) worried by the fear of suffering which (arises) from the discrimination (that) Saṃsāra (is distinct from the Absolute), do not know[29] that Saṃsāra and Nirvāṇa are identical. As (things which seem) real by discrimination have (in truth) no reality, they think that Nirvāṇa (is realised) through future abandonment of the senses and sense-spheres ... (They do) not (know that Nirvāṇa) is the Store-consciousness (*vijñānālaya*) which, after a reversal has taken place (in man), has itself for the final goal. Hence ... deluded men are adherents of a trinity of (Buddha) vehicles[30] (and) not adherents of the truth: '(Everything is) Mind only', which possesses no idols. Therefore ... those who have not understood the doctrine of the past, future and present Perfect ones, that all Objects are Mind itself, and who confess to the view that objects are something external to the Mind—(therefore they) enter again the wheel of the (imagined) Samsāra. (LS 2 p. 61 f.)

Saṃsāra and Nirvāṇa are in essence identical, for both are Mind: Saṃsāra as individuation and ideation, Nirvāṇa as Base-consciousness. Nirvāṇa is reached by way of 'reversal' (*parāvṛtti*), by turning away from the ideated world and individuation and by returning to the Base-consciousness as the Absolute.

So much for the *Laṅkāvatārasūtra*.

The Śāstras generally agree with the Sūtra, but differ in some details. Our presentation follows Vasubandhu's *Vijñaptimātratāsiddhi-Triṃśikā* and his *Trisvabhāvanirdeśa*. Difficulties in

[29] I read and Suzuki translates: *aviśeṣājñāḥ*.

[30] These three vehicles are: That of the listeners (*śrāvaka*) who owe their enlightenment to instruction by a Buddha; that of the Private Buddhas (*pratyekabuddha*) who have found enlightenment on their own, but do not preach the teaching; and that of the Bodhisattvas who exert themselves for the liberation of others. The two former vehicles belong to the Hīnayāna, the latter belongs to the Mahāyāna.

comprehending these texts arise mainly from the inconsistencies of their terminology.

In analogy to the doctrine of the Three Bodies Vasubandhu distinguishes—as the *Laṅkāvatārasūtra* did before him—three modes of existence (*svabhāva*), categories, or stages of being which he calls (a) the Absolute, (b) imagination and (c) the imagined. They are nothing but consciousness (*vijñāna*), yet in differing states of emanation and with different degrees of reality.

(a) The Absolute (*pariniṣpanna*) is identical with the Base- or Root-consciousness (*mūlavijñāna* [T 15] or *mūlacitta* [Tsv 29]) which is also called the Storehouse-consciousness (T 2) as it contains all karmic seeds (T 18). Whereas the Sūtras and Vasubandhu himself identify the Base-consciousness with the supreme reality and Thusness (T 25) and so regard it as uncreated and eternal, another verse of the *Triṃsikā* (19) describes it as the product of previous Karman. Hence it is also called (karmic) ripening (T 2).

By reason of the karmic seeds or impressions which are stored in the Base-consciousness and want to ripen, there arise in the Base-consciousness as coarsenings (T 29) the categories of (b) the dependent or imagination (T 21), and (c) of the imagined (T 20).

(b) The category of the dependent or of imagination (*vikalpa*) —also called thought (*manas*; T 5)—forms that which the worldling experiences as his ego, namely the person. It is the bearer of the process of imagination inasmuch as it ideates a world of objects by means of thought-activity (*manana*; T 5).

(c) The ideated world of objects constitutes the third stage of being, that of the imagined (*kalpita* [Tsv 1] or *parikalpita* [T 20]). The imagined is nothing but false idea (Tsv 4) and deception (Tsv 12); it does exist as appearance, but not as that which it seems to represent (Tsv 12).

The way in which the imaginary ego and its world arise out of the Base-consciousness can be depicted schematically as follows:

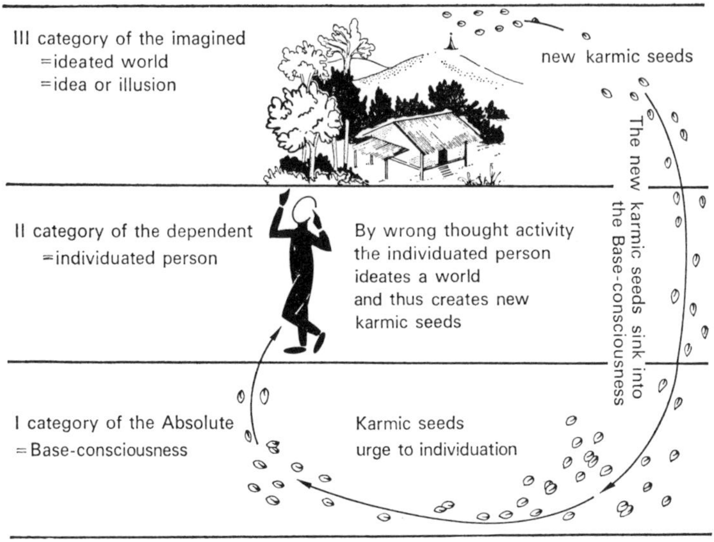

The *Trisvabhāvanirdeśa* contains a simile which is meant to elucidate the nature of the three modes of being and their inner relationship:

> When, through a spell, a magical object like (for example) an elephant, appears out of something (such as a piece of firewood), then (this) is a mere phenomenon (*ākāra*); there is no trace of a (real) elephant. (27)
> The category of the imagined is the elephant. The dependent is the phenomenon (*ākṛti*). The (essential) non-existence of the elephant is described as the Absolute. (28)

In the *Trisvabhāvanirdeśa* Vasubhandhu also deals with the way to liberation to which he pays no attention in the *Triṃśika*:

> In order to penetrate the True Nature (of things one has to reflect on) the Three Categories at the same time. Successively (one then develops) knowledge, renunciation, and attainment. (31)
> Knowledge is the non-perception (of any duality between

subject and object, i.e. insight into the ideatedness of the external world). Renunciation is described as the non-appearance (of future individuations). Finally, attainment (of liberation), has as its cause the perception (of the Absolute =Base-consciousness), which is immediate knowledge. (32)

V

THE TANTRAYĀNA AND THE BUDDHISM OF EAST ASIA

Hīnayāna and Mahāyāna, but not the other schools of Buddhism, can be described from the texts in Pāli and Sanskrit, but to study them presupposes a knowledge of Tibetan and Chinese and so goes beyond the competence of Indology. They are, therefore, only outlined here from secondary sources and in their ideal forms.

The Tantrayāna, 'Vehicle of the Tantra texts', is an occult Buddhism which arose in the second century A.D., made its literary appearance from the sixth century onwards, and in the eighth century found its way into the Buddhist universities as a subject on their curriculum. Only some of its sacred books, which are probably the oldest, survive in Sanskrit, but most of them are extant in Tibetan translations. The Tantra literature is still largely unexplored, not least because of its 'twilight language', which stands between light and shade, between assertion and concealment, and makes use of symbols difficult to understand.

Philosophically the Tantrayāna builds on the Mahāyāna but modifies or extends its principal tenets in several ways. It transforms the doctrine of the Three Bodies into a Four-Body doctrine by assuming a further body beyond the Dharmakāya; it divides the other Kāyas, as well as Emptiness, into subgroups or aspects; and introduces a great number of new psychological terms which largely defy translation into any Western language as they presuppose experience in meditation and thinking in other categories than the ones to which Westerners are used.

Four schools or methods for salvation have to be kept apart in the Tantrayāna: Mantrayāna, Vajrayāna, Sahajayāna, and Kālacakrayāna. They form the vertical division of the Tantrayāna and are on their part horizontally divided into four layers of realisation.

(1) The *Mantrayāna*, like all other Tantrayānic schools, is based on Mahāyānic monism. One has, however, to distinguish between classical and popular Mantrayāna.

Popular Mantrayāna interprets the essential identity of all beings with the Absolute as cosmical interrelatedness: nothing happens without some effect on everything else. The mistake of this conception lies in the fallacy that the identity-nexus which exists only in the sphere of the essential is also present in the area of the illusory. This leads to magic, for the interrelatedness of all things seems to make it possible to bring about any result by way of *mantras*, which here are understood as spells. Knowledgeable Tantrayānins reject this interpretation.

Correctly understood, *mantras* are syllables or sentences—usually without meaningful contents—which a spiritual preceptor (*guru*) imparts in secret initiation to his disciple after a long preparatory period, and which constitute the key by which the *sādhaka* (adept) can unlock in himself the door to the Absolute and thus to liberation. They have no outward effect but are a psycho-active medicine that works inwardly by leading to the experience of one's essential liberatedness. Of course, they can only do this if they are accompanied by concentration, a wholesome mental attitude and self-discipline, for they are unable to remove impeding Karman which obstructs the way to the liberating insight. Mantras are not the spells of a salvation magic.

A second instrument of the Mantrayāna are ritual gestures of the hands and fingers (*mudrā*), which amplify the efficacy of *mantras*. For as any emotion expresses itself in a specific bodily reaction, so, in reverse, the assumption of a certain body or hand posture can produce the corresponding psychical state.

(2) The *Vajrayāna* takes its name from the commonest of all Tantrayānic symbols, the *vajra* (Tib. *Dorje*). Originally the designation of the lightning-sceptre of the Vedic rain and storm god Indra, the texts of the Mahāyāna understand by *vajra* a super-natural substance, hard as a diamond, transparent as

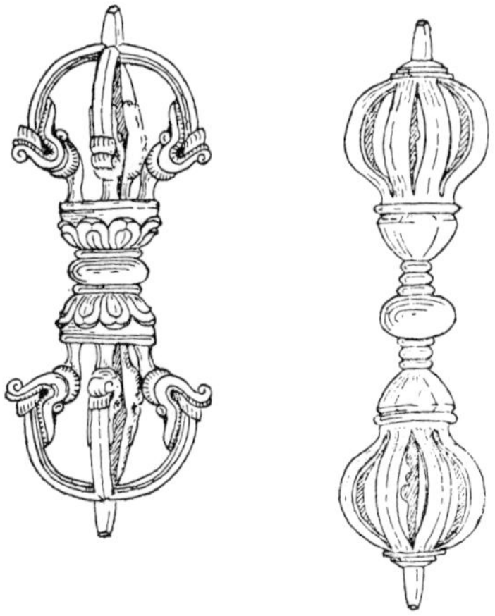

Two types of the Tibetan *vajra* (Tib: *dorje*) with four and eight outer bars respectively, plus the axis. The flattened ball in the centre symbolises Emptiness. The more frequent four-barred type has the Five Transcendent Buddhas (symbolised by the bars and the axis) ascending from emptiness through the lotus (=purity) and merge at the tip. Viewed from above the vajra forms a maṇḍala.

The symbolism of the eight-barred type is similar, but is modelled on a different maṇḍala, namely that of the Nine Transcendent Buddhas. Between the ball in the centre and the lotus flowers (worn on the specimen copied here) are three bulges symbolising the triple world which was born out of Emptiness.

empty space, and indestructible. The Vajrayāna applies the word to (i) enlightenment, in which man gains insight into his Emptiness (= Buddha nature), and to (ii) the Absolute Emptiness itself, which is also unshakable, indivisible, impenetrable, incombustible and indestructible. Finally (iii) *vajra* is the name of the ritual sceptre of the Vajrayānic monk which as Indra's lightning destroys the darkness (of ignorance).

The liberation method of the Vajrayāna proceeds from the conviction that for each human being the world of phenomena unfolds anew and individually from the Absolute as its 'seed' (*bīja*) as he, through his ignorance, imagines two things, namely the phenomenal world and deliverance, where in reality there is only One, namely the Absolute. Though each being is, in its core, identical with the Absolute, it possesses nevertheless an intrinsic individual nature which is expressible in a secret seed-

mantra (*bījamantra*). An initiate who knows the seed-formula of a Transcendent Buddha or Bodhisattva can by concentrated repetition of, and meditation on, this seed-formula call him out of the Emptiness into spiritual existence. He ideates and visualises him and thus creates for himself a spiritual guide who is always present, though visible only in meditation. The supermundane figures of the Vajrayāna are not objective realities, but 'accomplishings' (*sādhana*), that is subjective apparitions of the Absolute (= Emptiness = vajra = liberation).

In its conception of Transcendent beings the Vajrayāna is directly dependent on Yogācāra philosophy. According to the Yogācāra, the world which besets man so mercilessly is as much his mental creation as the fellow-beings whom he believes that he 'perceives'. It was but a small step for the Vajrayāna so to regard the Transcendent Buddhas and Bodhisattvas as well as ideations. There is only one difference between the ideation of a world from the ideation of Transcendent beings. The latter are not readily visible, because the ability to see them has to be acquired through spiritual practices. The world-ideation, on the other hand, is an effect of old Karman and automatically forces itself on to everybody.

For the Westerner, these thoughts are not easy to follow as he is accustomed to take as real only that which is objectively provable. He will dismiss as mere fancy a subjectively real being who is visible to its creator only, to the Sādhaka. The Vajrayānin, however, thinks differently. Reality is everything that is effective, no matter whether inwardly or externally, for one or for many. To the Sādhaka the visualised Transcendent being is no less real than is the physician for the patient, and it exercises the same function on a higher level. What difference does it make whether instructions about the way to salvation come from a *guru* or from a visualised Transcendent Bodhisattva? Quite to the contrary, the Bodhisattva embodies the Absolute more purely than the human teacher who is still affected by saṃsāric accidentals. The Bodhisattva's instruction, therefore, is of a higher, nay, the absolute, degree of truth.

The Sādhaka and the Transcendent Buddha or Bodhisattva

The Dharmakāya can be conceived as impersonal or personal. In the 10th century A.D. the Vajrayānins introduced the expression 'Primeval Buddha' and individualised him with a name. As Vajrasattva he holds the Vajra in his raised right hand and the bell in his left which is resting on his lap. The two ritual instruments symbolise Method and Wisdom, respectively Enlightenment and Compassion, the two indispensable conditions for deliverance. According to another interpretation the Vajra stands for eternity, the bell for impermanence, for the world is transient like the sound of a bell. (Tibetan wood-cut.)

ideated by him do not, of course, face each other as strangers. Knowing that the 'accomplishing' of a Transcendent being with all his perfections is his own ideation and hence part of himself, the Sadhāka performs the process of 'I-making' (*ahaṅkāra*), or 'identification'. He experiences the unity with the Buddha so vividly that he adopts that Buddha's qualities. Thus the identity with the Absolute, which was never really interrupted, again becomes part of the Sādhaka's vital consciousness. In Vajrayānic art the Absolute and the world of phenomena are symbolised as male and female figures. A couple in sexual union represents the Unio Mystica, in which the Sādhaka experiences the all-identity.

The abundance of supra-mundane beings in the Vajrayāna would have grown into anarchy if the most important Buddhas and Bodhisattvas had not been canonised and brought into a system. In the third/fourth century the scheme of the Five Transcendent Buddhas (see p. 108) was created. According to sectarian preference the one or other of the Five Buddhas

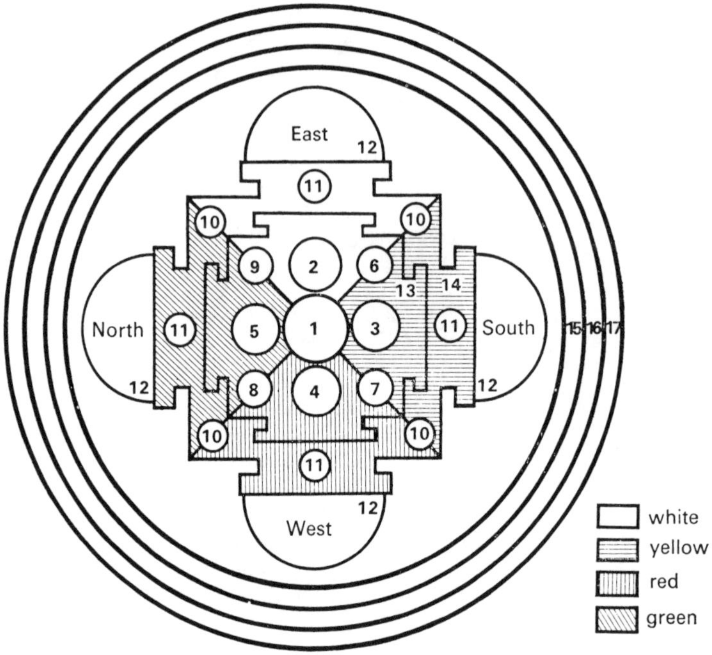

Maṇḍalas serve as aids to meditation and are: (a) ground-plans of the spiritual world and (b) depictions of the Mahāyānic way to deliverance.

In India meaning (a) is the dominating one which is why—in accordance with the indigenous geographers—the East is positioned at the top of the maṇḍala: the onlooker faces the rising of the sun. Many Tibetan maṇḍala artists on the other hand regard meaning (b) as more important; they position the East at the bottom of the maṇḍala: On his way to deliverance the believer follows the course of the sun.

The beings acting in the maṇḍala can be depicted graphically, or indicated by their symbols or seed-syllables. From the hundreds of maṇḍalas, the (simplified) *vajradhātumaṇḍala* has been selected here to explain the basic principles.

(a) In the centre of the world is the personification of the Dharmakāya: the Primeval Buddha (1), which rank in the present example is held by Vajrasattva. From him, four paradises, differentiated by colour, extend to the four directions. The Eastern Paradise (white) is presided over by the Transcendent Buddha Akṣobhya (2), the Southern Paradise (yellow) by Ratnasambhava (3), the Western Paradise 'Sukhāvatī' (red) by Amitābha (4), and the Northern Paradise (green) by Amoghasiddhi (5). At the sides of these Buddhas are the Transcendent Bodhisattvas who are assigned to them, namely Vajrapāṇi (6), Ratnapāṇi (7), Avalokiteśvara (8), and Viśvapāṇi (9). All these beings, which on Tibetan hanging scrolls are often surrounded by their mystic 'families', live in the sanctum that is indicated by the inner contour (13) which copies the ground-plan of a temple. Outside the sanctum in the 'palace' (14) dwell the Earthly or Human Buddhas (10) and the guardians (11). The latter are often deities of the popular religion which were adopted into Buddhism.

(b) As depiction of the way to deliverance the maṇḍala is to be 'read' from the circumference to the centre.

Attracted by the voice of an Earthly Buddha (10) which sounds out of the palace and discloses to him the path to deliverance, the salvation seeker first crosses the fire circle (17) of purification and then the Vajra circle (16) of initiation. His spiritual rebirth is symbolised by the lotus circle (15).

He now steps in front of one of the arched gates (12) where he has to account for his conduct of life to a guardian (11). If a remnant of impeding Karman blocks his entering, the Bodhisattva (6–9) takes the burden off him. Now the Transcendent Buddha (2–5) welcomes him into his paradise. Undisturbed by worldly influences he here matures to enlightenment, wisdom and the realisation of the Absolute. Through the uniomystica with the Primeval Buddha (1) he finally attains Nirvāṇa.

was elevated above the others, declared the personification of the Dharmakāya (= Vajra = Absolute), and put in the centre of the *maṇḍala*. Occasionally it is Akṣobhya, more often Vairocana, but usually Vajrasattva (*Whose Nature is the Vajra*) or Vajradhara (*Vajra bearer*) on whom the top position is conferred. In this case he replaces Vairocana. From the tenth century onwards, the designation 'Primeval Buddha' (*ādibuddha*) becomes customary for the personified Dharmakāya. The notion of the Primeval Buddha is said to have originated in the monastic university of Nālandā, possibly after the model of Islamic monotheism.

Once a hierarchy of supra-mundane salvation helpers had been established, it was but a small step to the idea of depicting the relationship between them in form of drawings. Monk-artists began designing *maṇḍalas* (lit. 'circles'): maps of the transcendent world, in which the Buddhas, Bodhisattvas and subordinate deities were distributed to the four cardinal points of the compass and their respective paradises. Naturally the Primeval Buddha as the personified Absolute resides in the centre. *Maṇḍalas* serve as aids for meditation, in particular in the monasteries of Tibet.

(3) The Sahajayāna, which apparently developed in the eighth century, bears quite a few resemblances to Zen-

Buddhism which, incidentally, in that century had followers in Tibet. Its most important text is the *Dohākośa* of Saraha(pāda) (eighth/ninth century), a collection of 280 stanzas which are extant in Tibetan and (fragmentary) in Apabhraṃśa, on the partial translation[31] of which the following paraphrase is based.

Mantras, Tantras, meditation and concentration, sings Saraha, only lead to self-deception (23); all schools of thought merely cause confusion (35). Neither the exclusive practising of Emptiness (70) nor clinging to this notion (75) nor renunciation of the world (10–16) lead anywhere. Deliverance is possible as a married householder (19), for the own body is a blessed shrine (48). The Buddha (68) and the Supreme One are in oneself (60). Why then renounce sensual enjoyment? Provided one does not get ensnared by attachment to the senses (71), they do not hinder liberation (19;24). The yogin at the root of things enjoys the material world, but is not enslaved by it (64).

The right way is, however, not found without instruction. Only at the feet of a *guru* is knowledge of the Absolute obtainable (17). Hence confidence is to be placed in his word (33).

It is wrong to regard sorrowful existence and liberation as essentially different. Saṃsāra and Nirvāṇa are the same (102). They are *sahaja*, 'twinned' (lit. 'born-together'), and do not exist side by side, but within each other. Not quite itself and not quite something other, the Twinned is neither existent nor non-existent (20). All diversities are thought-constructions (37); in reality Dharma is the same as Non-Dharma (3), for all things are one (26); everything is Buddha (106).

With regard to formal morality, the Sahajayāna way to liberation is characterised by unconstraint. The yogin has to devote himself to the welfare of others (112) and to cultivate compassion for all beings (107–110). He has to refrain from

[31] *Saraha's Treasury of Songs* (= Folk-Dohās), translated from the Tibetan into English by D. Snellgrove in *Buddhist Texts through the Ages* (Oxford 1954), text No. 188. The figures given in parentheses indicate the verses of this rendering. The forty King Dohās with commentaries have been translated by H. V. Günther, *The Royal Song of Saraha* (Seattle/London 1969).

vain discussion (55), for only if one is free from words can one understand words (88). In other respects he may live as he pleases (55); in order to obtain deliverance no outer discipline is necessary. The essence by which one is born, lives and dies, is also conducive to the attainment of the highest bliss (21). Deliverance is realised in self-experience (76).

However, the Sahajayāna demands great exertion in mental discipline which is based on the insight that all differences take their issue in thinking, are but forms of thought (37). Essentially, thinking is pure (23), but on account of karmic effects it ideates a world which possesses the nature of its owner (72). The liberation of thinking and the realisation of Nirvāṇa lie in release from Karman (40).

The inner discipline of the Sahajayāna can be summarised in the formula: know the mind, know your own thought (32). All diversity (37), Saṃsāra as well as Nirvāṇa, springs forth from mind (41). Only he who has realised the twinship (*sahaja* of Saṃsāra and Nirvāṇa) can acquire the absolute truth (13). The yogin has to hold fast to the (realisation of the) twinship (44), and regard all things as (essentially) alike (75). The world is enslaved by thought (78); only when the mind has ceased to be mind, does the true nature of the Twinned shine forth (77; 83). One has to renounce thought and adhere to singleness (55). The yogin has to become free from thought and like a child (57). When enlightenment is gained, where then is Saṃsāra, where Nirvāṇa? (103; 27). The sense-faculties of the Liberated One have come to a standstill, his notion of an I is destroyed (29). The liberated mind is tranquil (43); with a motionless mind one is released from the toils of existence (59).

Like other Tantrayānic schools the Sahajayāna represents the two pre-conditions to deliverance, Wisdom and Method, by the symbols of the *vajra* (male) and the lotus (female). In the union of both lies the bliss (94–95). Yogin and yoginī must unite, but only he who knows that everything is of his own nature will in the moment of embrace win the great bliss (91).

(4) The as yet little-explored *Kālacakrayāna*, which originated in the tenth century, is a system of astrology the elements

of which were raised into a religion. Man is conceived as an analogue to the cosmos; his physical and mental functions run parallel to the cosmic processes. The knowledge of the secret inner relations between man and the cosmos leads the initiate to liberation.

The word Kālacakra, 'Wheel of time', seems originally to have denoted the circle of the zodiac. The Kālacakrayāna understands the term, however, as the proper name of the Primeval Buddha who supervises the course of heavenly and earthly destiny. The Primeval Buddha Kālacakra is the spiritual centre of the system and forms the hub of numerous *maṇḍalas*. Mystical identification with him reveals to the follower all the knowledge which he needs for achieving the goal.

Through the four schools of the Tantrayāna run horizontal divisions into four levels of realisation. Above the *Kriyātantra*, 'ritual practice', which is followed by those who consider cult as decisive, ranks the *Caryātantra*, the 'practice of conduct' of those who regulate their daily life according to the Tantrayāna, but have only a faint idea of its deeper meaning. Next follows the *Yogatantra*, the 'practice of (mental) exertion', in which the adept strives for the spiritual contents of the Tantra. The crown of the system is the *Anuttarayogatantra*, the 'practice of supreme union': The adept realises the full meaning of the Tantrayāna and experiences the Absolute. Tibetan scriptures compare the four stages with the wooing between man and woman. The exchange of amorous glances is followed by smiling, grasping of the hands and finally the complete act of love. This comparison introduces further sexual symbols into the Tantrayāna.

The spread of the Tantrayāna in the sixth and seventh centuries coincides with the decline of Buddhism in India. From the eleventh century onwards Indian Buddhism lived in the shadows; in the thirteenth century it was practically extinct in the land of its origin. Internal and external reasons were responsible for this development.

Although the Tantrayāna may have cherished high ideals, many people felt repelled by the frequent excesses of its followers and by its symbolism which includes comparisons from the sexual sphere. Taking Tantrism for a degenerated religion, they transferred their antipathy to Hīna- and Mahāyāna as well. In the ninth century Hinduism launched a counter-attack. Buddhist ideas were deliberately incorporated into Hinduism and the historical Buddha declared an incarnation of the god Viṣṇu. What once had been attractive in Buddhism could now be found in Hinduism as well.

Indian Buddhism received its death-blow from Islam. As Gautama's doctrine relies on monachism and monasteries, it was unable to survive the forcible destruction of its Indian *vihāras* with their libraries and the slaughter of thousands of defencelessly surrendering monks between 712 and 1250. Its fate was sealed with the end of the Pāla dynasty of Bengal when it lost its last royal patronage. Among the 570 million inhabitants of India there are today as few as four million followers of the Buddha's doctrine—mainly former Harijans who in the Indian states of Mahārāshtra and Madhya Pradesh were won over to Buddhism by the social reformer Dr. B. R. Ambedkar (1893–1956) and the movement founded by him. The remainder are the adherents of the Mahā- and the Tantrayāna in the Indian Himālaya regions which are under the influence of Tibetan culture. A person who wants to study orthodox Theravāda has to go to Ceylon and South East Asia.

Of the East Asian variants of Buddhism, two are especially noteworthy: Amida (Skt. Amitābha) Buddhism—at home in China since the fourth century—which teaches liberation by the grace of Amitābha and was consolidated as a school by the Japanese masters Honen-Shonin (1133–1212) and Shinran-Shonin (1173–1262), and Zen (Jap.; Chin. *Ch'an*; Vietn. *Thien*). Zen is based on the teachings of the Yogācāra to which it gives a mystical interpretation and with which it combines Taoist ideas. It was founded in China around 520 by the Indian monk Bodhidharma and had its golden age between the eighth and thirteenth centuries. About 1200 it found its way also to Japan.

Zen turns against devotionalism and traditional religious customs. It throws off all intellectualism and all clinging to

Buddhist tenets in order to empty the mind for enlightenment (Jap. *satori*; Chin. *wu*), in which man awakens to the insight of the Buddha-heart, that is the essential identity of all things. All that exists is in essence Mind-only (= Buddha). On the question whether this enlightenment experience occurs suddenly like a flash of lightning or ripens slowly like a fruit, the two most important of the five Zen sects (Jap. *Rinzai* and *Soto*) hold different opinions.

As the way to enlightenment Zen teaches extensive meditation (Jap. *zen*; Skt. *dhyāna*). The Rinzai school, moreover, makes use of *koans*, which are questions meant to direct the seeker to the Unspeakable. In one *koan* a disciple asks the Chinese Ch'an master Hui Hai (eighth/ninth century): 'It is said that Mind is identical with the Buddha, but which of these is really the Buddha?' The master replies: 'What do you suppose is *not* the Buddha? Point it out to me!' As the pupil does not have enough *Zen* to answer the question, the master continues: 'If you comprehend (the Absolute Mind), the Buddha is omnipresent to you; but, if you do not awaken to it, you will remain astray and distant from him for ever.' The Chinese–Japanese tradition knows 1700 such *koans*. The oldest of them can be grasped intuitively, the younger ones are in every respect unintelligible. Their anti-logic is a pedagogical instrument. Reflection and meditation on such *koans* changes the Zen student's thinking to the point that the question finally ceases to provoke him, and so is 'solved'.

Zen training leads the student away from ignorance via the questioning of things to the insight of their thus-ness. As the Ch'an master Ch'ing-Yüan (eighth century) puts it:

> Before you study Zen, mountains are mountains and rivers are rivers. While you study Zen, mountains are no longer mountains and rivers no longer rivers. When you have obtained enlightenment, mountains are again mountains and rivers again rivers.

The goal of Zen is higher naturalness in the awareness of essential unity.

VI

A CULTURAL-HISTORICAL SURVEY

The Buddha was no prophet, but a sage and teacher, and that is what he took himself for. Nothing about him suggests prophetic possession by an overpowering numinous, nothing he ever said indicates a conviction of being the mouthpiece of a higher being. No dynamic obsession makes him try to change the world. He regards himself as a road sign to deliverance, appeals to man's intelligence and recommends adaptation to the natural laws of existence. His teaching addresses the individual, not an ethnic or racial group, and hence, in contrast to the ethnic religion of Hinduism it was able to win followers outside India as well and become a world religion.

To be interwoven with the cosmic cycle does not, however, mean to reconcile oneself to life's suffering. The idea that suffering is a trial is foreign to Buddhism. On the contrary: its aim is to vanquish suffering, and since it does not consider this possible by changing the outer conditions of existence, it teaches ways to obtain freedom from suffering through an expedient mental attitude. It is—as are all forms of mysticism—introversive and its way to salvation is psychological.

This conception results from a specific view of man. Man is not evil, but infatuated by egoism; his ignorance, not his depravity, involves him in suffering. He fares in the world like the little boy with bitter cod-liver oil. He took it only because for each spoonful his mother put a penny in his money-box. When the cod-liver oil was finished the box was opened and the money used for buying a new bottle.

Unlike the religions of Middle Eastern origin the idea of an almighty god does not play any role in Buddhism. Not god or gods (though such are recognised), but man is the object of

Buddhist thought. Although later Buddhist schools believe that outside assistance is possible, the last step to liberation has to be taken by each one himself. That Buddhism regards everybody as able to do this gives it, in the last analysis, an optimistic tendency.

I

As the Buddha teaches, everything existing has Three Marks: (a) impermanence, (b), sorrowfulness, and (c) non-selfness. Only that which is devoid of these three characteristics can be called of genuine value. Hence only deliverance, that is extinction (*nibbāna*) of the individuality, is true happiness.

(a) The whole universe is in a state of flux, in incessant change. Passing-away conditions new origination, origination leads to change and renewed passing-away. There is no constant being, only becoming; nothing *is*, everything *happens*. If existence were a permanent state of being, it would not be *life*.

This ceaseless change is perceived most distinctly in one's own course of life. Birth, ageing, illness and death are its phases. To a man who is greedily attached to things and to his supposed Self, impermanence causes nothing but suffering. The thoughtful observer, however, realises that it also opens up the way to dis-becoming, to liberation.

(b) 'Suffering' (*dukkha*) in Buddhist usage designates not only grief and pain; the term also includes the being exposed to an adverse environment, the being menaced by loss and transitoriness and the insecurity of momentary happiness. Due to their frailty even pleasant sensations and joys are sorrowful. 'Suffering' is a philosophical term and covers everything that is subject to the cycle of becoming and decay (*saṃsāra*); the adjective 'sorrowful' means unliberated.

(c) The world was of interest to the Buddha only in so far as it is reflected in the mind of an observer. He took it as an appearance and was not one of those who believe in a 'true being' or an Absolute behind it. Neither the objects nor their observer are or have a permanent Soul. To speak of an ego, a Soul or Self, is merely a linguistic convention and does not refer to an objective entity. The factors which compose our empirical person and personality can be classified into Five Groups (*khandha*). Death, the disintegration of these Groups, does not set a Soul free.

So much for the philosophical axioms of the Buddha. The remaining features of his doctrine are of a religious nature.

The transitoriness of existence, the Buddha continues, had to be welcomed if suffering were to cease with death. Yet this is not the case. Craving and ignorance do not permit man's annihilation in death: they effect his rebirth. As long as he has not achieved in himself the termination of these defilements he strays about in Saṃsāra.

Since Buddhism denies the existence of a Soul, it is wrong in this case to speak of Soul transmigration. However, what Buddhism does teach, is rebirth. Imagine a billiard-table with the balls on it. When you strike the first ball, the kinetic impulse is transferred to the second and to the third one without anything material moving from the first to the third ball. Similarly each form of existence conditions the succeeding one which then is considered as its rebirth. Yet no Soul transmigrates through the chain of rebirths. Between person A and its rebirth B there is no, not even a partial, identity, but a relation of Conditioned Origination and dependence. Person B is contingent on person A, nothing more.

Whether existence B will be more favourable for liberation or less so is not a matter of chance. Here, too, Conditioned Origination is at work. It is the deeds (*kamma*), consciously and intentionally performed, which determine the quality of the next form of existence. Wholesome action-intentions (*saṅkhāra* or *cetanā*) lead to a wholesome rebirth, unwholesome action-intentions to an unwholesome rebirth. It is up to each one to fashion his own future rebirths. If all his life a person has cultivated predominantly good action-intentions this will after his death result in 'his' attaining a good embodiment, perhaps as a god. Of course, existence as a god is not identical with liberation as the gods too will have to resign their position as soon as the good deeds, on account of which they attain godship, have worked off. Usually five realms of rebirth are distinguished. Rebirth into the world of man is regarded as the most favourable one because it offers the best prospects for deliverance.

When deeds are bound to lead to rebirth and even the most advantageous form of existence does not represent liberation, what then is the use of good deeds?

As the Buddha declares, a good form of existence provides better chances for rooting out the defilements which keep the cycle of rebirths in motion, namely craving and ignorance. Actions performed without greed, hatred and delusion do not entail rebirth effects. When Saṃsāra comes to a standstill for somebody, extinction of the sorrowful empirical individuality (i.e. liberation) occurs.

From these philosophical and religious premises the Buddha derives his ethics. Good, that is wholesome, are all those kinds of behaviour which weaken craving, hatred and ignorance:

> To abstain from all evil,
> to cultivate the wholesome,
> to purify one's mind—
> that is what the Buddhas teach. (Dhp 183)

According to the traditional view every person who follows the Eightfold Way to deliverance is a disciple of the Buddha, irrespective of whether or not he understands the theoretical part of the doctrine.

After the master's death monastic philosophers elaborated the doctrine of Conditioned Origination and developed it into a clear-cut theory. According to it all beings are composed of short-lived Conditioned Factors of Existence (P.: *dhamma*; Skt.: *dharma*), that is entities of various categories of thought which, through the formative power of Kamma, link up for some time to form those structures which we experience as 'I' and the world. Before long they disintegrate again in order to make room for new Dhammas and new Dhamma conglomerations. The process takes place on a smaller scale, so offering an explanation for the constant flux of our consciousness, the kaleidoscopic changing contents of mind, and our life processes—and on a larger scale where it serves to explain the process of rebirth without a Soul. In course of time the Dhamma theory became a central doctrine of Buddhism.

> Of the Dhammas proceeding from causes
> the Perfect One has told (us) the cause.
> And also their (possible) ending
> was taught by the great wandering monk—
>
> (Mv 1, 23, 5 I p. 40)

thus the monk Assaji defines the Teaching of his master. The stanza is accepted as a credo throughout the Buddhist world.

II

For Hīnayāna Buddhism the world is but appearance, and it denies that there is a thing-in-itself, an essence behind the phenomena. In the Buddha's understanding 'world' is that which is as such reflected in man's consciousness. Whether the sense-organs present a true picture of the external world never occupied his interest.

Mahāyāna Buddhism, arising about the first century B.C., draws far-reaching conclusions from this conception.

If the empirical world, so it says, is a mere phenomenon of which we can never be sure to receive a faithful image through our sense-organs, then we are entitled to regard it point-blank as illusion. What, however, is illusory and lacks an individual ego or Soul is in other words empty (*śūnya*). Consequently Emptiness (*śūnyatā*) is the essence of the world of phenomena: The attributeless Absolute of all empirical beings and things. The assertion of an Absolute, for which the Mahāyāna presumably took as model the upaniṣadic *brahman* teaching which the Buddha had once rejected, brings Mahāyāna Buddhism into philosophical opposition to Hīnayāna.

The Illusory and the Absolute are, however, not separated, but interwoven, for which Tantrayāna Buddhism later coins the term 'twinned' (*sahaja*). The Absolute is inherent in illusory 'reality'; Saṃsāra and Nirvāṇa are basically the same. In the illusory sphere beings are different and separated, in their Emptiness as the Absolute they are identical. And since the Absolute is liberation, they are in essence also free—a fact of which the majority of people are unaware. To realise liberation requires merely a change of mental attitude. He who has seen through the illusoriness of suffering and become conscious that his own Emptiness is identical with the Absolute (i.e. deliverance), can no longer be confused by the hazards of existence. As a sage, mentally aloof from the world, he lives in inner freedom and serenity towards Perfect Extinction.

The devaluation of the empirical world as illusory is also of consequence for the devotional Ways of the Mahāyāna. For the laws observed in the sphere of the illusory are now likewise regarded as illusory. At any time they can be thrown over by higher realities in which the Absolute is less concealed by accidentals. Rebirth determined by deeds—in Hīnayāna regarded as an iron law of nature—softens in Mahāyāna and thus makes it possible to assume that Transcendent Bodhisattvas and Buddhas can give the liberation-seeker assistance from outside. The recognition of such transcendent beings is the most obvious characteristic which distinguishes between Mahāyāna and Hīnayāna.

In the Mahāyāna system the term 'Bodhisattva' denotes beings who through the termination of greed, hatred and delusion have achieved deliverance, but due to their compassion for unliberated beings accept the Active Nirvāṇa only, a state of liberation which enables them to continue work for the good of the world. Not until all beings have been freed from suffering will they enter the Static Nirvāṇa which renders them ineffective for the world. They are not transcendent as if they were beyond all experience; they are merely out of sight for the every-day man. Advanced liberation seekers are able to perceive them. Whenever a call for help is sounded, be it in distress or out of the desire for deliverance, the Transcendent Bodhisattvas, who are no longer subject to the laws of nature,

Kuanyin (=Chin; Jap. Kannon), the East Asian form of Avalokiteśvara. Although essentially male, he can—like all Transcendent Bodhisattvas—also assume female shape for the purpose of granting assistance. Hence, East Asian art often depicts him as a madonna. (After a Chinese wood sculpture of the Sung period [960–1279].)

will rush to assist. Some Mahāyānic schools look at the Transcendent Bodhisattvas as ideations of one's own consciousness: helpers of subjective reality who can be physically effective.

Of the same nature as these Bodhisattvas are the Transcendent Buddhas who, through the annihilation of the factors causing suffering, have worked their way up to their present rank. They do not, however, take part in worldly affairs, but are primarily keepers of paradises, sorrow-free realms into which all those are reborn who through their faithful confidence attract the grace of a Transcendent Buddha. The sojourn in such a paradise—the most popular of them being the Pure Land of Amitābha which is situated in the West—is not identical with deliverance. Rather the follower matures there in the wisdom and knowledge which he needs to reach Nirvāṇa. To some Mahāyānins the Transcendent Buddhas and their paradises are also nothing but ideations.

The Mahāyāna does not stop at declaring the world to be illusory. In the fourth century the Yogācāra school springs up which carries the idealisation further. It appraises the empirical world not only as illusion but as a projection of one's own consciousness. The Dharmas which compose our personality and our empirical world are flashes of consciousness. The world is merely ideated and the empirical personality nothing but a karmically conditioned idea in the universal Base-consciousness (*ālayavijñāna*). He who has seen through this is liberated, for in the moment of his insight the world with its empirical suffering and the supposed Self are, for him, dissolved.

III

The Tantrayāna probably originated in the second century A.D. Philosophically it has added little to Buddhism; its contribution lies in the psychological sphere.

In their quest for liberation Mantra- and Vajrayāna make use of language in the form of meaningless syllables, the so-called *mantras*. Mantras are the psycho-active medicine against the feeling of isolation from which all our suffering stems: the fallacy that individual consciousness and Base-consciousness (= deliverance) are separate and different. Without disturbing the intellect they dis-inhibit the 'psyche' for the experience of universal One-ness in the Essential. As every *mantra* is only wholesome for a certain person or type of person and perilous for others, they are kept secret.

Taken in a double dose, namely as seed-formulas (*bīja-mantra*) they lead the mind to ideate subjective transcendent salvation helpers. The adept feels himself so vitally one with the Bodhisattva or Buddha whom he has ideated and visualised that he adopts emotively the Bodhisattva's state of liberation and in this way vividly experiences what has existed from the beginning: essential identity between himself and the Absolute, between individual consciousness and Base-consciousness, between Saṃsāra and Nirvāṇa.

The Sahajayāna is a reaction to the frequent misuse of *mantras*. It rejects the mantric method and tries to obtain the experience of the 'twinship' of suffering and liberation by means of insight alone. Its disregard for external observances and systematical discursive thought gives it an intuitionist character.

IV

Whereas the history of Buddhist thought presents itself to the philosophical observer as a gradual idealisation of the empirical world, comparative religion looks upon it as a series of attempts to reach by different routes Nirvāṇa, which in all schools of Buddhism remains the goal of deliverance. Four of the seven ways to deliverance can already be proved in Hīnayānic texts.

(1) The Way of Self-discipline is the oldest of them all. It is effective for liberation because it destroys the basic defilements, namely craving and ignorance, hatred and delusion, which cause karmic bondage to Saṃsāra. Some Mahāyānic schools raise objections against this Way. To follow it, they say, demands too much of an ordinary human being, and it is a slow and egoistic method of salvation. The Tantrayāna, particularly in its form as Sahajayāna, understands self-discipline as an inner discipline and considers this alone as decisive. Outer discipline, it holds, is of little importance.

(2) Meditation after various methods is extensively described in the Pāli texts. Originally an aid to the destruction of greed, hatred and delusion, it later developed into an autonomous Way to deliverance. In some schools of meditation based on Pāli scholasticism and in Zen it is the exclusive instrument of liberation.

(3) The value of wisdom is emphasised in the Pāli canon dozens of times. For good reason, since Wisdom is the antithesis of ignorance which is the cause of suffering. Yet a real Way of Wisdom can only be spoken of after the arising of Hīnayānic scholasticism, which, however, very often regards as Wisdom the having by heart of as many texts and Abhidhamma formulas as possible. The Way of Wisdom is indeed of paramount importance in the *Prajñāpāramitā* literature of the Mahāyāna, and in the Madhyamaka school which is based on it. This school—in consequence of its monistic outlook—confers a new significance on Wisdom: awareness of one's own

identity with the Absolute and of one's essential liberatedness.

(4) The Bodhisattva Way, that is confidence in the Bodhisattvas' readiness to help the seeker to achieve salvation, presupposes a conviction foreign to the Pāli texts, of the transferability of karmic merit. To accept the assistance of the Bodhisattvas puts the seeker under the moral obligation to strive himself for Bodhisattvahood in order to help liberating other beings from suffering. Bodhisattvahood as religious goal is so typical of the Mahāyāna that in its texts it often refers to itself as the 'Vehicle of the Bodhisattvas'.

(5) The Way of Devotion or Faith begins historically in the middle-Hīnayānic period, but it was only the Mahāyāna that canonised it as faithful devotion to the Transcendent Buddhas. The gracious Buddhas cannot lead the believer directly to liberation, but merely to rebirth in a paradise where he then matures to Nirvāṇa.

(6) The Cultic Way—a concession to the piety of the masses—has its roots in the worship of relics, *stūpas*, and (in later times) Buddha images and is first mentioned in the *Mahāvastu*. The view that the ritual, even when performed absent-mindedly, leads automatically to enlightenment (= deliverance) is, however, exclusively Mahāyānic and a deviation from the basic conviction of all the other ways to liberation.

(7) The Tantrayāna adds to these the Way of Mantras which enables the adept to experience and realise the all-identity.

V

In the two-and-a-half thousand years of its history the Teaching of the Buddha has travelled a long way. From Afghanistan to Japan, from Mongolia to Ceylon and Java, men have professed to it, and to a large extent still do so today. Whatever culture it came in touch with, its influence was always ennobling. Thousands of monasteries, temples and Stūpas, even if partly in ruins today, covered with sand or overgrown by jungle, tell the story of its peaceful victory. The wheel of the Dharma continues to turn, somewhat creakingly, under the burden of our extrovert industrial civilisation and the impact of materialist doctrines, but it turns. Will it come to a standstill?

The style of our life has changed in the last decades, but the hearts of men have remained the same. No less strong than the urge for prosperity, joy and progress, is the longing for a glance beyond into the realm of the timeless. The heavier the present weighs on man, the more he listens to the voice of silence. And hence there will always be at least a few who hear and understand the word of the Buddha: about the Way towards the termination of suffering.

Despite all the knowledge which we possess and can master only with the help of machines, we cannot cope with ageing, death and transitoriness. Our knowledge and actions move in the realm of the finite. Can we afford to disregard the Infinite as it can be divined in the Teaching of a compassionate sage?

VII

TABULATED SYNOPSIS

Branch	*School (as far as mentioned in present book)*	*Period and country of Origin*	*Founder or Systematiser (as far as mentioned in present book)*	*Language of Oldest Original Sources*	*Still Extant in*
Hīnayāna	Original Buddhism (in all central doctrines presumably identical with Theravāda)	6th cent. B.C. in India	Siddhattha Gotama, the 'Buddha' (563–483 B.C.)	Māgadhī(?) (no written sources)	—
	Theravāda	4th cent. B.C. in India	Separate school from Second Council onwards	Pāli	Ceylon, Burma, Thailand, Laos, Cambodia, Vietnam
	Mahāsāṅghika	4th cent. B.C. in India	Separate school from Second Council onwards	Hybrid Sanskrit (only fragments)	—
	Puggalavāda	3rd cent. B.C. in India		Pāli(?)	—
	Sarvāstivāda	3rd cent. B.C. in India	Vasubandhu (5th cent. A.D.)	Sanskrit (only fragments)	—
	Sautrāntika	2nd cent. B.C. in India		Sanskrit (only fragments)	—
Mahāyāna	Wisdom School	1st cent. B.C. in India		Sanskrit	Tibet, Nepal, Sikkim, Bhutan, Vietnam, China, Korea, Japan
	Madhyamaka	2nd cent. A.D. in India	Nāgārjuna (2nd cent. A.D.)	Sanskrit	As above
	Bodhisattva School	1st cent. A.D. in India		Sanskrit	As above
	Buddhism of Faith	1st cent. B.C. in India	In Japan: Honen-Shonin (1133–1212), Shinran-Shonin (1173–1265)	Sanskrit	As above

Method for Achieving Deliverance	*Interim Goal*	*Ultimate Goal*
Termination of rebirth through eradication of the causes of rebirth and suffering, viz. craving and ignorance, by means of self-discipline and enlightenment	—	a) Pre-mortal Nibbāna b) Post-mortal Nibbāna
As above	—	As above
As above	—	As above
As above	—	As above
As above	—	As above
As above	—	As above
Realisation of the emptiness of the empirical person and of all things and insight by means of Wisdom, that this Emptiness is the Absolute and liberation	—	a) Pre-mortal Nirvāṇa b) Post-mortal Nirvāṇa
As above	—	As above
Relief from unwholesome Karman through the assistance of Bodhisattvas	Out of gratitude for the help received from Bodhisattvas to become oneself a Bodhisattva in order to help others	a) Active Nirvāṇa b) Passive Nirvāṇa
through faithful confidence in Transcendent Buddhas (esp. Amitābha) to obtain rebirth in a Buddha paradise	Rebirth in one of the Buddha paradises (esp. Sukhāvatī) where the faithful mature toward Nirvāṇa	Nirvāṇa

Branch	School (as far as mentioned in present book)	Period and country of Origin	Founder or Systematiser (as far as mentioned in present book)	Language of Oldest Original Sources	Still Extant in
Mahāyāna —*cont.*	Yogācāra	3rd/4th cent. A.D. in India	Maitreyanātha (3rd/4th cent.) Asanga, Vasubandhu (4th/5th cent.)	Sanskrit	Tibet, Nepal, Sikkim, Bhutan, China, Japan
	Zen (Ch'an)	6th cent. A.D. in China	Bodhidharma (6th cent.)	Chinese	China, Vietnam, Korea, Japan
Tantrayāna	Mantrayāna	2nd cent. A.D. in India		Sanskrit	Tibet, Sikkim, Bhutan, Mongolia, China, Korea, Japan
	Vajrayāna	3rd cent. A.D. in India		Sanskrit, Tibetan	Tibet, Sikkim, Bhutan, Mongolia, China, Korea
	Sahajayāna	*c.* 8th cent. A.D. in India	Sarahapāda (8th/9th cent. A.D.)	Apabhramśa, Tibetan	Tibet, Sikkim, Bhutan, Mongolia
	Kālacakrayāna	10th cent. A.D. in India		Sanskrit, Tibetan	As above

Method for Achieving Deliverance	*Interim Goal*	*Ultimate Goal*
Realisation that everything is 'Mind only' and return to the Pure Mind (= liberation)	—	Nirvāṇa
Realisation by means of meditation that everything is 'Mind only' (= Buddha Heart = liberation)	—	a) Pre-mortal Nirvāṇa b) Post-mortal Nirvāṇa
Deliverance through knowledge of the identity of individual consciousness and Base-consciousness by means of psychologically effective Mantras and Mudrās	—	As above
Through seed-formulas the Sādhaka ideates Transcendent (Bodhisattvas) with whom he emotively identifies himself. He so experiences the essential all-identity and becomes aware of his essential liberatedness	—	As above
Through discarding vain thinking which is the cause of multiplicity, the Yogin intuitively grasps the interwovenness of Saṃsāra and Nirvāṇa and by this realises liberation	—	As above
Liberation through the realisation of the parallelism between man and cosmos. The mystical union with the Primeval Buddha Kālacakra reveals all the insights important for liberation	—	As above

VIII
LITERATURE

1. *Abbreviations and Text Editions*

A	Aṅguttaranikāya, PTS edition
Ak	Abhidharmakośa (of Vasubandhu), ed. by R. Sāṅkṛtyāyana, Vārāṇasī 1955
AP	Aṣṭasāhasrikā-Prajñāpāramitā, ed. by P. L. Vaidya, *Buddhist Sanskrit Texts*, vol. 4, Darbhanga 1960
Bca	Bodhicaryāvatāra (of Śāntideva), ed. and transl. into Hindī by Śāntibhikṣuśāstri, Lucknow 1955
Chin.	Chinese
Cv	Cullavagga of the Vinayapiṭaka
D	Dīghanikāya, PTS edition
Dhp	Dhammapada
Itiv	Itivuttaka, PTS edition
Jap.	Japanese
Khp	Khuddakapātha, PTS edition
Kr	Karatalaratna (of Bhāvaviveka), re-translated from the Chinese into Sanskrit (and furnished with a summary in English) by N. Aiyaswami Sastri, in: *Visva-Bharati Annals*, vol. 2, Santiniketan 1949, pp. 35 ff.
Kv	Kāraṇḍavyūha, ed. by P. L. Vaidya in: *Mahāyānasūtrasaṅgraha*, Part I, *Buddhist Sanskrit Texts*, vol. 17, Darbhanga 1961, pp. 258 ff.
LS	Laṅkāvatāra-Sūtra, ed. By B. Nanjio, *Bibliotheca Otaniensis*, Kyoto 1956
LSsag	Sagāthakam (= appendix in verses) to the LS
M	Majjhimanikāya, PTS edition
Mś	Madhyamakaśāstra (of Nāgārjuna with Candrakīrti's commentary), ed. by P. L. Vaidya, *Buddhist Sanskrit Texts*, vol. 10, Darbhanga 1960
Mv	Mahāvagga of the Vinayapiṭaka, PTS edition
Mvś	Mahāyānaviṃśikā (of Nāgārjuna), Sanskrit text (with

	English translation) in: G. Tucci, *Minor Buddhist Texts*, Part I, *Serie Orientale Roma*, vol. IX, Rome 1956
P	Pāli
PH	Prajñāpāramitā-Hṛdayasūtra, Sanskrit text (and English translation) in: E. Conze, *Buddhist Wisdom Books—The Diamond Sūtra and the Heart Sūtra*, London 1958
PTS	Pāli Text Society, London
S	Saṃyuttanikāya, PTS edition
Skt	Sanskrit
Snip	Suttanipāta, PTS edition
SP	Saddharmapuṇḍarīkasūtra, ed. by N. Dutt, *Bibliotheca Indica*, Work No. 276, Calcutta 1953
Śs	Śikṣāsamuccaya (of Śāntideva), ed. by P. L. Vaidya, *Buddhist Sanskrit Texts*, vol. 11, Darbhanga 1961
SvL	Sukhāvatīvyūha (longer recension), ed. by P. L. Vaidya in: *Mahāyānasūtrasaṅgraha*, Part I, pp. 221 ff. (see Kv)
T	Triṃśikā (of Vasubandhu); edition: *Vijñaptimātratāsiddhi* (with Sthiramati's commentary), ed. by Swāmī Maheśvarānanda, Vārāṇasī 1962
Thag	Theragāthā, PTS edition
Tib.	Tibetan
Tsv	Trisvabhāvanirdeśa; edition: *The Trisvabhāvanirdeśa of Vasubandhu*, Sanskrit Text and Tibetan Versions, ed. with an English translation by S. Mukhopadhyaya, Visvabharati Series No. 4, Calcutta 1939
Ud	Udāna, PTS edition
Vin	Vinayapiṭaka, PTS edition
Vism	Visuddhimagga (of Buddhaghosa), PTS edition
VP	Vajracchedikā Prajñāpāramitā, ed. and translated into English by E. Conze, *Serie Orientale Roma*, vol. XIII, Rome 1957

2. *Translations of Indian works; Secondary Literature*

As the present work does not contain any quotations from secondary literature, a list of the books consulted was dispensable. It may be mentioned, however, that the selection of references was considerably eased by the anthologies of Warren (1896), Oldenberg (1922), Seidenstücker (1923), Woodward (1925), Winternitz (1929+30), Conze (1954+9), von Glasenapp (1956), and Frauwallner (1958).

For further studies in Buddhism the reader is referred to

S. Hanayama, *Bibliography on Buddhism*, Tokyo 1961.

C. Regamey, *Buddhistische Philosophie* (Bibliographische Einführungen in das Studium der Philosophie, vol. 20/21), Bern 1950.

The following list names some scientifically based and recommendable recent works.

The life of the Buddha in history and legend is retold in:

A. Foucher, *La Vie du Bouddha d'après les textes et les monuments de l'Inde*, Paris 1949 (abbr. English edition: *The Life of the Buddha*, Middletown/Conn. 1963).

The various systems of Buddhism are outlined in:

A. Bareau a.o., *Die Religionen Indiens*, vol. 3: Buddhismus, Jinismus, Primitivvölker (Die Religionen der Menschheit, vol. 13), Stuttgart 1964.

E. Conze, *Buddhism—Its Essence and Development*, Oxford 1957.

E. Frauwallner, *Geschichte der indischen Philosophie*, vol. 1, Salzburg 1953.

R. A. Gard (ed.), *Buddhism*, New York/London 1961.

K. W. Morgan (ed.), *The Path of the Buddha—Buddhism interpreted by Buddhists*, New York 1956.

W. Rāhula, *What the Buddha taught*, Bedford 1967.

R. Robinson, *The Buddhist Religion—A Historical Introduction*, Belmont (California) 1970.

Bhikshu Sangharakshita, *A Survey of Buddhism*, Bangalore 1966.

Bhikshu Sangharakshita, *The Three Jewels—An Introduction to Buddhism*, London 1967.

A. K. Warder, *Indian Buddhism*, Delhi 1970.

The conception of Nibbāna is examined on the basis of the Pāli Nikāyas in:

R. E. A. Johansson, *The Psychology of Nirvāṇa*, London 1969.
A system of Buddhist meditation with a compilation of illustrating Hīnayānic and Mahāyānic texts is given in:

E. Conze, *Buddhist Meditation*, London 1956.

A presentation of the Mahāyānic Way to deliverance is found in the following book which is a translation of a Tibetan text of the twelfth century A.D.:

H. V. Guenther, *The Jewel Ornament of Liberation* (by sGam. po. pa), London 1970.

An idea of the Prajñāpāramitā literature and its philosophy is conveyed in

E. Conze, *Selected Sayings from the Perfection of Wisdom*, London 1955.

E. Conze, *Buddhist Wisdom Books—The Diamond Sūtra and the Heart Sūtra*, London 1958.

E. Conze, *Aṣṭasāhasrikā Prajñāpāramitā* (English translation), *Bibliotheca Indica*, Work No. 284, Calcutta 1958.

Important contributions to our knowledge of the two philosophical Mahāyāna schools are:

K. K. Inada, *Nāgārjuna—A Translation of his Mūlamadhyamakakārikā with an Introductory Essay*, Tokyo 1970.

T. R. V. Murti, *The Central Philosophy of Buddhism—A Study of the Mādhyamika System*, London 1960.

K. Venkata Ramanan, *Nāgārjuna's Philosophy as presented in the Mahā-Prajñāpāramitā-Śāstra*, Rutland/Vermont/Tokyo 1966.

R. H. Robinson, *Early Mādhyamika in India and China*, Madison/Milwaukee/London 1967.

F. J. Streng, *Emptiness—A Study in Religious Meaning*, Nashville/New York 1967 (contains translations of the *Madhyamakaśāstra* and the *Vigrahavyāvartaṇī*).

A. K. Chatterjee, *The Yogācāra Idealism* (Banares Hindu University Darśana Series, vol. 3), Banares 1962.

Of the Tantras only the following is available in a European language:

D. L. Snellgrove, *The Hevajra Tantra—a Critical Study* (London Oriental Series, vol. 6), London 1959.

Useful for the knowledge of Tantrism are:

A. Bharati, *The Tantric Tradition*, London 1965.

Lama A. Govinda, *Foundations of Tibetan Mysticism*, London 1959.

Compilation: *The Cultural Heritage of India*, particularly vol. 1, pp. 486–536 and IV pp. 211–279, Calcutta 1958 and 1956.

G. Tucci and W. Heissig, *Die Religionen Tibets und der Mongolei* (Die Religionen der Menschheit, vol. 20), Stuttgart 1970.

Apart from the works of D. T. Suzuki the following book on Zen is recommendable:

J. Blofeld, *The Zen Teaching of Hui Hai on Sudden Illumination* (a treatise and a collection of sayings of the Zen master H.H. who lived in the eighth/ninth century A.D.), London 1962.

History and spread of Buddhism are outlined in:

E. Conze, *A Short History of Buddhism*, Bombay 1960.

E. Zürcher, *Buddhism—Its Origin and Spread in Words, Maps and Pictures*, London 1962.

The most comprehensive modern compendium of Buddhism which examines its origin, councils, spread, legends, schools, canonical languages and changes in contents up to the first century A.D., by making use of almost all primary and secondary sources, is:

É. Lamotte, *Histoire du Bouddhisme Indien—des Origines à l'Ère Śaka* (Bibliothèque du Muséon, vol. 43), Louvain 1958.

Information on Buddhism in Germany is supplied in:

H. W. Schumann, *Buddhism and Buddhist Studies in Germany*, Godesberg 1972.

Index

Compiled by the author.

The plates are indicated by an 'a' following a number, i.e. 64a is the plate opposite page 64.